The Prisoner of St Kilda

The Prisoner of St Kilda

The true story of the unfortunate Lady Grange

MARGARET MACAULAY

Luath Press Limited

EDINBURGH

www.luath.co.uk

First published 2009

ISBN: 978-1-906817-02-2

The paper used in this book is sourced from renewable forestry and is FSC
credited material.

Mixed Sources
Product group from well-managed
forests and other controlled sources
www.fsc.org Cert no. SA-COC-1565
© 1996 Forest Stewardship Council
FSC

The author's right to be identified as author of this book under the Copyright,
Designs and Patents Act 1988 has been asserted.

The publisher acknowledges subsidy from

Scottish
Arts Council

towards the publication of this volume

Printed in the UK by MPG Books Ltd, Cornwall

Typeset in 11 point Sabon

Map by Jim Lewis

© Margaret Macaulay 2009

For Christina, Henri and Niall

Contents

Acknowledgements

I have pursued Lady Grange through collections, archives, and published material. En route I have become indebted to a great many people, including the staff at the National Library and the Map Library in Causewayside. The Special Collections Department of Edinburgh University Library generously granted access to the Laing Collection and the hoard of treasures hidden under the prosaic cover of La.11. 201. It was an unforgettable experience to hold in my hand the only surviving original letter of Lady Grange's from St Kilda, and to have it reproduced for this book.

For advice on available portraits thanks are due to the staff of the National Portrait Gallery, the National Gallery of Scotland and its Picture Library, and to the National Trust for Scotland for the portrait of Lord Dun. James Erskine, 14th Earl of Mar and Kellie provided unrestricted access to the family portraits at Alloa Tower and those on loan to the Portrait Gallery, as well as to his family's papers in the National Archives at Register House. For permission to reproduce the sketch of the old St Kilda village by Sir Thomas Dyke Acland, I am grateful both to Sir John Acland and to the Royal Commission on Ancient and Historical Monuments of Scotland.

My personal thanks to my editor, Jennie Renton, my family for their support, and to Professor Murdo Macdonald for helpfully suggesting sources of Highland views and providing his own photographs of Glencoe, Castle Tioram and Assynt.

I would also like to express my indebtedness to Michael Robson, author of the magisterial *St Kilda: Church, Visitors, and 'Natives'*, whose painstaking research into Church of Scotland and sspck records provides previously unexamined evidence on the work of these organisations in the time of Lady Grange.

Picture Credits

Portraits reproduced with the kind permission of the National Galleries of Scotland: Lord Grange, on long-term loan from the Earl of Mar and Kellie; Lady Grange, on long-term loan from the Earl of Mar and Kellie; Simon Fraser, Lord Lovat; Norman MacLeod 22nd Chief of Clan MacLeod.

Portraits reproduced with the kind permission of the Collection of the Earl of Mar and Kellie, Alloa Tower: Sir Hugh Paterson; Lady Jean Paterson; John Erskine, 6th Earl of Mar with son Thomas; John Erskine, 6th Earl of Mar, in exile; Frances Pierrepoint with daughter Frances; John Francis Erskine and family.

National Trust for Scotland: David Erskine, Lord Dun.

Edinburgh University Library, Special Collections Department: facsimile of Lady Grange's letter from St Kilda (Laing Collection Div. 11, No. 201).

The sketch by Sir Thomas Acland of village of St Kilda in 1812 is reproduced by permission of Sir John Acland.

Thanks are also due to the Trustees of the National Library of Scotland for permission to reproduce sections from the Pont map 32 of the East Central Lowlands and from the map of the Battle of Tranent (Acc. 8392).

Photographs: Glencoe, Tioram, and Assynt – Murdo Macdonald; Village Bay, St Kilda – Christina Macaulay; Cleit 85, grave-stone at Trumpan, and cover image – the author.

Chronology of Events

1679	4 February, baptism of Rachel Chiesley (Lady Grange)
	12 October, birth of James Erskine (Lord Grange)
1688	Catholic monarch James II deposed by his Protestant son-in-law, William of Orange
1689	Jacobites win the Battle of Killicrankie but their leader Viscount Dundee is killed and the Rising subsides
	31 March, Murder of Sir George Lockhart in Edinburgh by Lady Grange's father, John Chiesley of Dalry
	3 April, John Chiesley executed
1707	Marriage of Rachel Chiesley and James Erskine (approximate date)
	Union of the Parliaments
1710	Lord Grange appointed Lord Justice Clerk of Scotland
1715	George I succeeds to the throne; dismisses John Erskine, 6th Earl of Mar, Lord Grange's elder brother
	Jacobite Rising led by John Erskine, 6th Earl of Mar
1716	Rising suppressed and the 6th Earl of Mar goes into exile; the earldom is forfeited
1727	Smallpox outbreak on St Kilda kills two-thirds of the population
1730	Separation agreement between the Granges
	In the years running up to the '45, Jacobite meetings thought to have been held at Preston House
1732	22 January, Lady Grange forcibly removed from Edinburgh
1732–34	Lady Grange held on Heskeir, in the Monach Islands
1734	Lord Grange elected to Parliament at Westminster
1734–41	Lady Grange held on St Kilda
1740	Letters from Lady Grange arrive in Edinburgh
	Late in 1740 or early in 1741 Lady Grange removed from St Kilda to Assynt
1741	The sloop *Arabella* fails to find Lady Grange in the Hebrides
1745	Lady Grange's death on Skye
	Lord Grange marries Fanny Lindsay, his London mistress
	4 September, Charles Edward Stuart declares his father, the

Old Pretender, to be the King

17 September, Jacobite army led by Charles Edward Stuart takes Edinburgh

21 September, decisive win for the Jacobite army at the Battle of Prestonpans; a number of Government soldiers die trapped against the walls of Preston House

15 November, Carlisle falls to the Jacobites after a five-day siege

4 December, Jacobite army reaches Derby but with promised French and English military support not forthcoming, returns to Scotland

1746   17 January, Jacobites defeat Government forces at Falkirk

16 April, defeat at the Battle of Culloden brings the '45 to an end and Bonnie Prince Charlie flees to the Continent

1754   20 January, Lord Grange's death in London

1788   Death of Charles Edward Stuart in Florence

1824   Earl of Mar title restored to the Erskine family

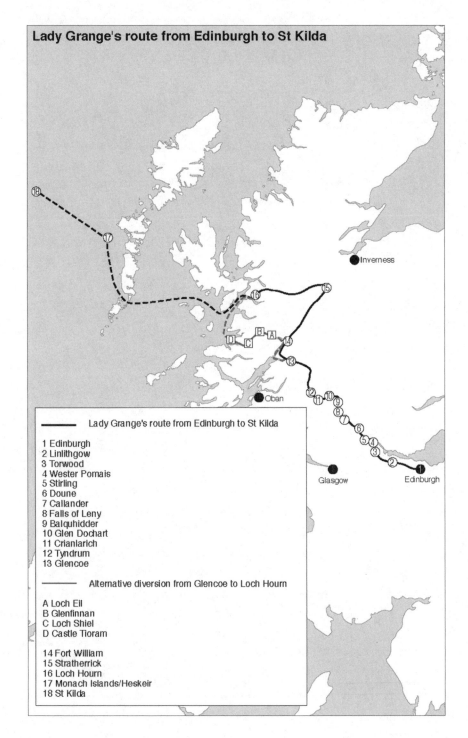

Lady Grange's route from Edinburgh to St Kilda

Lady Grange's route from Edinburgh to St Kilda

1 Edinburgh
2 Linlithgow
3 Torwood
4 Wester Pomais
5 Stirling
6 Doune
7 Callander
8 Falls of Leny
9 Balquhidder
10 Glen Dochart
11 Crianlarich
12 Tyndrum
13 Glencoe

Alternative diversion from Glencoe to Loch Hourn

A Loch Eil
B Glenfinnan
C Loch Shiel
D Castle Tioram

14 Fort William
15 Stratherrick
16 Loch Hourn
17 Monach Islands/Heskeir
18 St Kilda

Should you be in Edinburgh and wish to call upon Lady Grange or her husband Lord Grange, they can both be located in the Scottish National Portrait Gallery in the elegant New Town area of that city. Sometimes they are available without prior appointment. In that eventuality they are to be seen in the 18th century section of the gallery, among bewigged grandees and full-bosomed ladies. But sometimes a special appointment is required, since an over-abundance of past posers compete for the available wall-space. Then you must seek the Granges in the cold store.

'That's lucky,' said the attendant. 'They're both in the same one.'

'I'm not sure they'd like that,' I felt impelled to reply.

Rachel Chiesley, Lady Grange
(1679–1745). Portrait c.1710
attributed to
Sir John Baptiste de Medina.

James Erskine, Lord Grange (1679–1754).
Portrait by William Aikman, 1720.

PREFACE
A Strange Coupling

The true story of this Lady is as frightfully romantic as if it had been a fiction of a gloomy fancy.
Journal of a Tour to the Hebrides, James Boswell

IT WAS INDEED a strange coupling. James Erskine and Rachel Chiesley, Lord and Lady Grange, were uneasy bedfellows even at the best of times – which is hardly surprising if you give credence to contemporary gossip that he had been forced to marry her at the point of a gun, pressed to his head by the lady herself, and that she kept a razor handy under her pillow to remind her fickle husband of her tempestuous nature and her lineage as the daughter of a convicted murderer.

Yet who would blame Lady Grange if she eventually considered herself the wronged party? An imperious lady, she felt keenly her exclusion from the management of her husband's estate when he began to spend increasing amounts of time in London. Even more wounding was the knowledge of a mistress in the south.

As the relationship deteriorated James found his own unique solution. Making use of a mafia of male friends who shared with him an interest, to put it no higher, in the seditious business of Jacobitism, he arranged for the permanent removal of his wife. On 22 January 1732 Rachel was abducted from her lodgings in Edinburgh. Sentenced without trial, she spent the next 13 years on a variety of Scottish islands, the greater part of that time on St Kilda, the *ultima Thule* of Scotland.

Lady Grange never did succeed in returning home or seeing her family again. Nine long years would elapse before any communication at all from her would arrive in Edinburgh to alert her friends to the fate that had befallen her. Although a rescue ship was hurriedly organised, it was doomed to fail. Her captors, secure in their own familiar territory, would always be one step ahead of any attempt at rescue. Lady Grange was hastily removed from St Kilda in the winter of 1740–41, taken to a safe house in Assynt, then to Harris, and finally to Skye where she died in May 1745.

To our modern way of thinking James Erskine's solution to his marital problems may appear barbarous and cold-blooded. After 25 years of marriage and nine children, Rachel was simply erased from Edinburgh society and removed from its civilised comforts. Why was she treated so savagely? Did she in any way deserve her fate? Her story is so tragic in human terms, so intriguing in its intermesh with the politics of the period that it clamours to be re-examined. A visit to the National Portrait Gallery seemed a sensible first step to take in my journey to discover the true story of the celebrated and unfortunate Lady Grange.

CHAPTER I

The Cold Store

This matrimonial connection was far from agreeable to the Mar family and
ultimately turned out in every respect unfortunate.
'Memoir of Lord Grange', James Maidment

IN THE COLD STORE the atmosphere was appropriately frosty as the
gallery attendant pulled out one of the large support panels which
accommodate temporarily unwanted portraits. Not only were the
Granges in the same room but they shared the same panel. Eye contact
had however been avoided since Lord Grange's commanding full
length portrait was occupying a sizeable part of one side of the panel,
with Lady Grange's more modest head-and-shoulders oval painting
consigned to the other side.

Lady Grange was painted by John de Medina in 1710. She was then
about 31 years old – although her actual date of birth is unknown, her
baptism in Edinburgh is recorded on 4 February 1679, a ceremony
which normally took place soon after birth. In her portrait she looks
out at us with composure, a calm expression in the brown eyes, a hint
of a smile about the mouth.

If the tempestuous nature of which she was regularly accused is true,
Medina has failed to capture it. Her shoulder-length hair is dark and
a few stray curls cross the forehead. Rachel Chiesley was considered
something of a beauty in her early years, even by those who had little
else good to say of her. Yet here too Medina fails to provide the evidence.
The face is pleasant enough, but lacks any defining characteristic or
any striking feature. There is a certain blandness to the portrait which
puzzles and disappoints.

Lady Grange is wearing a rose-pink stole over a blue dress. The scoop neckline is edged with lace to demure effect. Perhaps the demureness was deliberate. Perhaps she was happy to promote the appearance of conformity and respectability, knowing how tongues had wagged only a few years earlier over her marriage to Lord Grange. And does the hint of a smile on her lips suggest the cat that has got the cream? After all this was 1710, the year when her husband, at the remarkably early age of 30, had been made Lord Justice Clerk of Scotland. Rachel Chiesley, whose father was publicly hanged in Edinburgh in 1689 for the murder of another law lord, had indeed achieved a remarkable success in society from a most ill-starred beginning.

On the other side of the hanging panel Lord Grange towers down, resplendent in his judicial red robes. At his side a table supports what are presumably some law books – legal knowledge literally at his slender, aristocratic fingertips.

Lord Grange's portrait was painted by William Aikman in 1720 when its subject was 40 years of age. James Erskine, second son of Charles, Earl of Mar, owed much of his early and swift rise in the legal profession to the powerful position in Queen Anne's government in London of his elder brother, John. This relationship would later turn out to be a mixed blessing, but while John was influential in London, James's legal career in Scotland flourished. Called to the Scottish Bar in July 1705, he was raised to the Bench as Lord Grange only a year later. From 1710 to 1714 he was Lord Justice Clerk, losing this position only when his brother fell from favour with the accession of the Hanoverian George I.

Worse, however, was to follow. John, nicknamed 'Bobbing John' for his facility to change political allegiance, made the disastrous decision in 1715 to return to Scotland and attempt to revive the cause of the deposed Stuart monarchy. The Jacobite Rising was an abject failure and Bobbing John paid a heavy personal price. Defeat at the Battle of Sheriffmuir led to the forfeiture of the earldom and exile on the Continent. He attempted a reconciliation with George I and several petitions were made on his behalf, all unsuccessful. John died in exile in Aachen in 1732, held in suspicion by both the Hanoverians and the Jacobites.

James Erskine had acted as chief factor for the Mar estates in the good days while his brother was Secretary of State in London. Family loyalty and no doubt a certain self-interest motivated him to continue looking after the affairs of his brother in exile, although he was well aware of the danger of being himself tainted with suspicion of Jacobitism. No longer Lord Justice Clerk, he continued to act as a judge in the Court of Session in Edinburgh.

When Aikman was commissioned to paint his portrait Lord Grange was a prominent figure in Scottish society, sharing with his contemporaries an interest in religious discussion and the business of the General Assembly of the Church of Scotland. He was settled happily into family life, at least to surface view, with a country house at Preston, near Prestonpans, and a townhouse in the capital.

For both Grange and Aikman, as indeed for all the members of what constituted the chattering classes of 18th century Scotland, the Union of the Parliaments in 1707 was beginning to have an effect. Looking towards London as the centre of power and influence – which had begun in 1603 with the departure south of the Scottish king and court – accelerated after the Union. Aikman himself was on the point of moving to London when Grange's portrait was painted.

James Erskine still foresaw his future in Edinburgh in 1720. Fourteen years would pass before he would begin to think seriously of a political career at Westminster, by which time he would have 'solved' the problem of a troublesome wife. Of more immediate concern to James was the need to look after the Erskine family interests in the absence of brother John without himself becoming suspected of sedition.

In the Aikman portrait Lord Grange stands comfortably shod in black, square-toed shoes with sensible, sturdy heels. He has the air of a man who knows how to tread a line without losing his balance. It would indeed be a pity if such a spotless pair of shoes, so symbolic of a successful lifestyle, were to be caught straying into undesirable company. Mud sticks, even to the shiniest of shoes.

CHAPTER 2
Murder in the Royal Mile

The character of the Assassin was shown by his demeanour when he was apprehended. On hearing that his victim had almost instantly expired, he declared, with savage exultation, that 'he was not used to do things by halves.'
An Account of the Assassination of Sir George Lockhart,
Hay's Manuscript, 1700

ALTHOUGH RACHEL CHIESLEY was only ten years old when her father, John Chiesley of Dalry, was convicted of murder and hanged in full view of the Edinburgh populace, the sins of the father were never entirely forgotten and were revisited whenever it suited anyone to denigrate the daughter. Chiesley was a man with a low flashpoint, quick to take to the law even against his own family, and quick to take the law into his own hands. If it had not already been appropriated by his native country, 'Wha daur meddle wi' me?' might have been minted as his motto.

His marriage to Margaret Nicholson had been an unhappy one, finally ending in separation. Margaret took him to court for maintenance for herself and their ten children – there is a suggestion that the children were starving – and at the final court hearing Sir George Lockhart of Carnwath, Lord President in the Court of Session, found against Chiesley, awarding Margaret alimony of 1,700 merks – approximately 93 pounds Scots per annum. Chiesley, incandescent, accused Lockhart of having taken the government of his family from him and threatened that, in the absence of 'a speedy remedie', he would attack Lockhart 'either in kirk or mercat'.

Lockhart's failure to take this threat seriously was a fatal mistake. He was shot by Chiesley as he walked home from church on Easter Sun-

Sir George Lockhart of Carnwath (c.1630–1689).

day, 31 March 1689. The murder took place in the High Street in the presence of several witnesses, including the victim's brothers.

The High Street and the Canongate form the greater part of what is popularly known as the Royal Mile, linking Edinburgh Castle at its head with the royal residence of Holyroodhouse at its foot. In summer its pavements are thronged with tourists and during the Edinburgh Festival a section of the street is pedestrianised to give performance space for human statues, jugglers, and hopeful young thespians in costume pressing flyers into the hands of passers-by. But on that March day in 1689 the street theatre was for real. No one was acting and no one had read the script beforehand.

Richard Augustin Hay has left us a vivid account of the assassination and the events leading up to it. It would appear that Chiesley had been stalking his victim. In a manuscript penned eleven years after the events described, Hay writes that the day before the murder Chiesley had been seen following Lockhart from the Duke of Hamilton's apartments at Holyroodhouse. The next day, outside the New Church (one of the smaller churches contained at that time within St Giles Kirk), Chiesley had offered money to the 'bedler' for a place in the seating area belonging to Lord Castlehill, the Lord President's brother, which would have positioned him strategically just behind his intended victim.

It is hard to credit that Chiesley actually intended to shoot Lockhart while he was at worship in a crowded church, yet that does seem to have been his intention. Informed that the particular seat he wanted was not available, Chiesley refused any other, reportedly pacing up and down till the sermon was over and walking out of the church ahead of Lockhart. He then stationed himself at the close entrance which he knew led down to the Lord President's house.

Edinburgh's Old Town was a crowded rabbit warren of wynds and closes leading off from the Royal Mile. High life and low life co-existed there, often sharing the same tenement stair, with the lower orders occupying the less salubrious apartments. There was a degree of social intercourse which would be lost when the upper classes decamped to the Georgian splendours of the New Town.

As well as the tenement 'lands' so characteristic of the Old Town, substantial townhouses were tucked away down the various closes and wynds. Lockhart lived in such a townhouse in Hope's Close, a short distance up the High Street from St Giles. He was accompanied on what would be his last walk home by his two brothers, Lord Castlehill and Daniel Lockhart.

We learn from a letter the Earl of Errol received a few days after the murder from a correspondent in Edinburgh, that the brothers discussed the sermon they had just heard delivered by Dr William Hay, Bishop of Murray and that the Lord President discoursed all the way about the sermon, asserting that 'he had nevir heard tell of so excellent a preacher before'.

It would have been strange if the conversation had not eventually turned to the subject of the political upheaval which was then convulsing both Scotland and England. William of Orange had landed in Devon the previous November and since Christmas King James II of England and VII of Scotland had been in exile in France, never to return to either country again. On 13 February William and Mary had been proclaimed joint sovereigns in London. The English had decided: the English Revolution was over. Scotland still hesitated. Claverhouse, Viscount Dundee, had been in Edinburgh earlier in the month before riding north to raise support for James. Even now, as the Lockhart party progressed up the High Street, the Castle at the top was still holding out for James. Scotland would decide on the 4th of April and the Scottish crown would be offered to 'the Prince and Princess of Orange, now King and

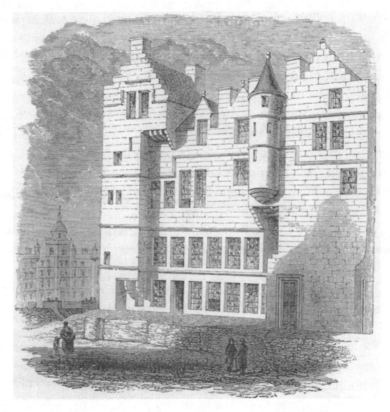

Sir George Lockhart's town residence in Hope's Close, Edinburgh. The close was demolished in the 1830s to make way for George IV Bridge.

Queen of England'; by which time, both Lockhart and Chiesley would be dead. That Sunday morning Lockhart's thoughts might well have turned to his wife, Philadelphia, who was ill at home. The doctor was due to call that very day to see her. Thinking of her, he might even have quickened his step. At the entry to Hope's Close, Chiesley saluted the Lord President and was acknowledged in return. Lockhart was a courteous man. He had discounted Chiesley's threats as idle bluster, even though friends had warned him to take care. His companions walked part-way down the close with him, engaging in a few last moments of conversation before bidding him farewell and walking back up towards the street. Lockhart had a second thought and called back to them. Daniel was returning when he encountered Chiesley.

'I thought you had been at London,' said Daniel Lockhart.

'I'm here now,' was the terse rejoinder.

Chiesley brushed past Daniel, who had put out his hand to greet him, caught up with Lockhart and discharged his pistol into his back. The bullet passed through Lockhart's body, fatally wounding him, before being battered on the close wall. Lockhart had time only to turn round and look his murderer in the face, before falling back against the wall. Too late, his companions rushed to his aid. 'Hold me, Daniel, hold me,' were the Lord President's last words.

CHAPTER 3
Dead and Buried

Lockhart was the most learned lawyer and the best pleader I have ever
known in any nation.
History of My Own Times, Bishop Gilbert Burnet

The fate of Chiesley was a sufficient warning to anyone who should dare to
assume the office of avenger of his own imaginary wrong.
The Bride of Lammermoor, Sir Walter Scott

CHIESLEY MADE NO attempt to escape and was immediately apprehended.
Retribution was exacted swiftly: murder on 31 March was followed
by trial and conviction on 1 April. As the crime had been committed
within the city of Edinburgh, the trial was held before the Lord Provost,
Sir Magnus Prince, as High Sheriff, sitting with James Graham, John
Charteris, Thomas Young and William Paton, city bailies. The jury
consisted of ten landed gentlemen and five merchants. Chiesley freely
confessed, adding that he had committed the murder because the
deceased had given an unjust sentence against him. According to the
account in Arnot's *Criminal Trials*, he was then asked if it was not
a sentence pronounced in favour of his wife and children, 'for their
aliment'? To which Chiesley's only response was that he would not
answer 'to that point nor give any account thereof'.

Despite his confession, it was decided that Chiesley should undergo
the additional torment of the 'boots' and 'thumekins' to determine if he
had acted alone or had an accomplice. If Chiesley has any redeeming
feature it could be said that even under torture he refused to implicate
anyone else. Thus the skin of a lawyer, Calderwood by name, was
saved. Calderwood had been seen at the Abbey the previous day in

the company of Chiesley and again at Hope's Close at the time of the murder. Inflamed with the righteousness of his cause, Chiesley may not have felt inclined to share the glory with anyone. The sentence pronounced was that on Wednesday 3 April he would be taken from the Tolbooth of Edinburgh, and dragged on a hurdle the short distance along the High Street to the Mercat Cross. There between the hours of two and four in the afternoon his right hand would be cut off before he was hanged on a gibbet. The pistol with which he had fired the fatal shot would be placed round his neck and his body taken to be displayed in chains between Leith and Edinburgh. His right hand would be fixed to the town's West Port and his moveable goods confiscated. All of which was duly carried into effect.

The Tolbooth would continue to serve as the town prison until it was demolished in 1817. It had earlier had a prouder history as the meeting place of the town council, the courts and even the Scottish Parliament, but it is its darker side as a prison that prevails in the collective memory of Edinburgh citizens. A heart-shape in the cobblestones around St Giles marks the site of the doorway through which so many, including John Chiesley, passed to their death.

On the day before his execution Chiesley would presumably have had a regulation visit from men of the cloth anxious over the health of his eternal soul. It seems hardly likely that Margaret Nicholson or any of his children took the opportunity for a final farewell to their *pater familias*. But Chiesley was still a man of social standing. The public display of his body in chains was uncomfortably close to the family mansion. Though spiked heads and hands as well as dangling corpses were not uncommon features of Edinburgh's street furniture in the late 17th century, Chiesley was spared the final lingering indignity that had been decreed for him. Friends quickly cut down his body from the gibbet and carried it away. On the same day as the execution, permission was granted by the town council for the interment of Lockhart's body within Greyfriars Kirk. According to council records, the Lord President's death was 'an inexpressible losse to this Kingdome'. Even hostilities were put on hold as the defenders of Edinburgh Castle requested a temporary truce for Lockhart's funeral. His memorial in the south-east corner of Greyfriars, reputedly the most imposing within

The Edinburgh Tolbooth, the town prison in the late 17th century.

that church, was destroyed by fire in 1845 but some lines from the inscription survive, translated into verse from the original Latin:

> So falls our glory with one fatal blow,
> Gone is that head which did us justice show.
> That tongue from which such well-tuned words did come,
> And charmed us all, is now for ever dumb;
> His pointed wit did in us hopes create
> To see our Church healed, and our tottering state;
> This stroke doth make them vanish into air,
> Leaves us behind to languish in despair.

So much damage to the body politic of Scotland, and all over the vexed question of alimony.

More than a hundred years after the murder of Lockhart, Sir Walter Scott was in conversation with a James Walker, then proprietor of Dalry House. Walker rightly thought that Scott might be interested to learn that during improvement work a skeleton had been uncovered, together with some fragments of iron. Scott reported the discovery in a letter to the secretary of the Society of Antiquaries of Scotland in Edinburgh. Despite the heinous nature of his crime, it would appear that John Chiesley was brought back home, albeit to an unmarked grave.

31

CHAPTER 4

Marriage

It was rumoured that the espousals were brought about by the Lady, who
having formed a pretty correct estimate of the fickleness of the gentleman, very
adroitly brought matters to a crisis, by presenting a pistol to her lover, and
bidding him remember that she was a daughter of John Chiesley of Dalry.
'Memoir of Lord Grange', James Maidment

He told me he loved me two years or he gott me and we lived 25 years
together few or non I thought so happy.
Letter from St Kilda, 20 January 1738, Lady Grange

MAIDMENT, WHO EDITED and published extracts from one of Lord
Grange's diaries in 1843, writes that James had 'previously slighted'
Rachel, which sounds like genteel Victorian-speak for that sin beloved
of old presbytery records, namely pre-nuptual fornication. James
and Rachel were hardly exceptional in this behaviour, and shotgun
marriages were not uncommon and could turn out well. It is in fact
highly unlikely that any gun ever featured in the proceedings.

The Mar family were less than enthusiastic over the union. The
Chiesleys were not of the first water, even discounting the blemish
of a murder conviction. As Alexander Carlyle, son of the minister at
Prestonpans, waspishly points out in his *Autobiography*, the Chiesley
knighthood dated back only to the time of Charles 1 and 'being a new
family they must have had few relations'. Few that counted, he means.
But Chiesley's brother Robert recovered well enough from the family's
misfortunes to be knighted and become Lord Provost of Edinburgh in
1694, and his eldest son, who inherited the family estate, served as a
major in the British army.

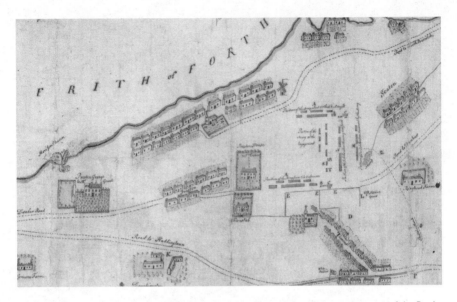

Preston House, country home of the Granges, is at the centre of this contemporary map of the Battle of Tranent (Prestonpans), fought to the east of the house on 25 September 1745.

The Granges settled down to married life, dividing their time between their Edinburgh townhouse and their country estate at Preston, within comfortable commuting distance of the capital. Carlyle, who knew the Preston gardens well, writes that Lord Grange brought them to perfection by having hedges of common elder planted as protection against the westerly and south-westerly winds. When these trees had grown to over 16 feet in height, the interior grounds were sheltered completely. The gardens were a copy in miniature of those at the Erskine family seat at Alloa, both being rich in 'close walks, and labyrinths, and wildernesses'. The Alloa gardens were described by Daniel Defoe in 1723 as 'by much the finest in Scotland and not outdone by many in England'. Visiting gardens was much in vogue in the 18th century and the Preston gardens became a popular destination for the curious who flocked from Edinburgh to admire them in the summer months on Saturdays and Mondays – though naturally not on Sundays, in sabbatarian Scotland. Apparently it took upwards of two hours to walk through the policies at Preston and crowds continued to come till 1740 – by which time the former lady of the mansion house had been a prisoner for over six years on the windswept, treeless island of St Kilda.

CHAPTER 5

The Granges at Home

I have reason to thank God that I was put out from the office of Justice-
Clerk for, besides many reasons from the time... this one is sufficient, that I
have thereby so much more time to employ upon God and religion.
Extracts from the Diary of a Senator of the College of Justice, Lord Grange

NO DOUBT ABOUT it, James Erskine was a religious man, and possibly
keen to underline that fact to anyone who might chance to read his
diary. For a glimpse into the early married life of the Granges the diary
is invaluable, even though it is a narrow glimpse, limited to the period
1717–18 and seen only through the prism of Lord Grange and his
interests. It is revealing not only for what he mentions to excess but
also for what he scarcely mentions at all.

Maidment confesses no desire to take on any of the other volumes of
the diary: 'Judging the remainder of the Diary by the portion perused,
it must be exceedingly dull and unreadable,' he writes. 'The endless
religious controversial disputations, not to mention the frequent
repetition of pious ejaculations, are tiresome in the extreme.' Yet
careful sifting of the predominantly religious content reveals personal
nuggets which are more fun to examine, psychology being a much less
dusty pursuit than theology. Every so often the man himself emerges
and the unavoidable adjective which springs to mind to describe him
is *incorrigible*.

Though Grange admits to many misdemeanours, or perhaps because
he does so with such candour, it is difficult to be censorious. He is always
full of good intentions. He means to pray more for his son, he means to
learn Hebrew in order to understand the Scriptures. He is so willing to

acknowledge that he is a sinner that even when the gardener purloins some of the produce from the Preston gardens for his own use, Grange decides that the gardener should be given the opportunity to return the stolen goods without losing his job, since he considers himself as guilty as his gardener in committing many ills. He confides to his diary that there was a time when he 'drank and whored' and followed sensual pleasures. He recalls that in Utrecht, years earlier, he had been laid low with 'a distemper that whoremasters seldom miss'. He admits that when he receives a legacy from a relative, 'she had previously had a just aversion to him, having seen him very beastly drunk'. Now, however, he is a reformed character. Ever since his attendance at communion in Prestonpans parish in the summer of 1716, he has acquired an aversion to those 'gross sins', which had been 'hard to forbear'. By May 1718 he is lamenting that he has 'religion enough to spoill my relish and prosecution of this world, and not enough to get me to the next'. A common enough complaint. We must surely sympathise. In fact Grange is so willing to admit his own fallibility that he comes across as quite an agreeable chap. Always supposing you are fortunate enough not to be married to him.

His family are mentioned only fleetingly. Rachel comes to Edinburgh on one occasion to visit him when he is taken suddenly ill there. She tells him their son, Charlie, was very affected to hear of his illness. Grange's response is to write to Charlie and exhort him to make sure he has an interest in God. There is mention of another son, ill with smallpox; Grange's chief concern for him is that, because of his illness, Jammie is being kept more among the hands of women and servants, 'hearing their foolish notions'. So now we know his opinion of women.

Then there is the sad fate of little Meggie. She arrives at Preston from Edinburgh with the rest of the family in February 1717, indisposed, but not dangerously, with teething problems. Leeches are applied to the child's neck. Unfortunately one makes a 'ragled' wound, which festers. The infection spreads over Meggie's neck and down her shoulders. The child lingers on, suffering greatly, before dying on 22 May. In December of this same year, which was so blighted by Meggie's dreadful illness and death, another daughter, Jean, is born. No sympathetic comment is elicited by his wife's suffering, losing one child and bearing another in such a short space of time. Even darker times lie ahead, foreshadowed in the diary. Mr Allan Logan, minister of the gospel at Culross, writes to Grange warning him to be on his guard and to be sure that the Government cannot lay anything to his charge. Grange is flattered by Logan's concern – especially as he thinks it might be God-inspired – and assures the minister that he is safe enough, although there are those in the Government with designs against him. Logan continues to be Grange's close friend. They have much in common, including a shared belief in the existence of witches. Visitors to the village of Culross on the north shore of the River Forth can still visit Logan's church today. In his time the church tower was used as an overflow prison for witches when there was no more room for those unfortunate women in the attic of Culross Townhouse.

Grange's country estate in present-day East Lothian was itself in an area renowned as a hotbed of witches. Scotland was one of the last countries in Europe to give up their persecution: as late as 1727 Janet Horne, an elderly woman possibly suffering from dementia, was tarred and feathered and paraded round the town of Dornoch in a barrel before being burned alive. Grange never lost his belief in their existence and many years later, when he became a Member of Parliament, he used his maiden speech to oppose a Bill then going through the House to abolish the statutes against witchcraft.

The diary also records the anxiety of a friend who has had a dream of Grange driving a cart along a road. In the dream Grange comes to a great 'hoall'. The wheel of the cart goes down the hole but doesn't break; Grange goes on to drive up an impossible precipice and in among some houses and then disappears out of sight. Beneath the calm surface of Grange's public life there appear to be undercurrents which are causing alarm to his friends, perhaps even to Grange himself.

His private life too may be under strain. Mr Cumming, the children's tutor, had been loaned a book by Lady Grange: *Annotations on the Holy Bible* by Matthew Poole. Grange records going to the tutor's room to retrieve it. There he comes across the young man's diary and has no compunction about reading it. He is duly rewarded by learning little good of his family: his son is a perverse pupil and his wife imperious with an unreasonable temper. Moreover Cumming had been warned when he was first coming to Preston that he would have many difficulties to grapple with. Grange suspects the source of that warning to be Mr Spark, the previous tutor, who stayed only half a year and 'did not behave as he ought'.

It looks as though the Granges have been having staff problems. Imperious ladies are not the easiest of employers. Imperious ladies can also be dangerous if they insist on sharing the driving seat on the family cart. What if Lady Grange should grab the reins just when Lord Grange wanted to be particularly careful about the route he was taking? The impossible precipice of his friend's dream might not be so easily negotiated. It might turn out to be the death of him.

CHAPTER 6

The Cracks Widen

Lord Grange was not unentertaining, in conversation, for he had a great
many anecdotes which he related agreeably, and he was fair-complexioned,
good-looking and insinuating.
Autobiography, Alexander Carlyle

She was gorgeously dressed, her face like the moon, and patched all over,
not for ornament, but for use. For these eighty years I have wandered in this
wilderness I have seen nothing like her... She appeared to me to be the lady
with whom all well-educated children were acquainted, the Great Scarlet
Whore of Babylon.
Autobiography, Alexander Carlyle

ALEXANDER CARLYLE WAS not born until 1722 and so his memories of
the Grange family, and particularly of Lady Grange, are the memories of
a child. But what a wide-eyed, open-eared, taking-everything-in child.
From the manse pew every Sunday he would observe the landed gentry
and the lesser locals. At home he listened to, but never interrupted, the
conversation of his parents. That way he learned and retained a lot.
When he came to write his autobiography in old age he revisited those
early years, recalling the local scene and the family life of the Granges
in colourful episodes which remained unfaded in his memory despite
the passage of years.

There was, for instance, the occasion when Colonel Charteris, the
celebrated gambler, came to his father's church in Prestonpans, in the
party of Morison, owner of Prestongrange estate. Carlyle tells us he
was five or six years old at the time, so this must have been around
1728. All the young Carlyle knew of Charteris was the popular opinion
that he was a wizard with some fascinating power. 'I never took my

eyes off him during the whole service,' he writes in his *Autobiography*, 'believing that I should be a dead man the moment I did.'

Lady Grange of Preston House was another of the congregation who kept a watchful eye on all that happened in the kirk. On one occasion she felt obliged to complain to the minister about the inappropriate behaviour of his young son, whom she had detected smiling at her son John, who was about the same age. Even more shocking, Alexander had been trying to write with his finger on a dusty desk in front of him instead of paying attention to the sermon. Carlyle does not tell us what action, if any, his father took to punish such behaviour, but Lady Grange's intervention affected Carlyle's attitude to her, long after dusty desk-tops had ceased to hold any attraction for him.

Only a few days after the incident in the church, the paths of the lady and the young lad crossed again, providing Alexander with yet another source of grievance. He had wandered some distance on his own from the manse and had reached the Red Burn, which at that time divided Prestonpans from its suburbs, the Cuthill. He was happily hovering on the bank of this stream, considering whether to try crossing, when Lady Grange passed in her coach. Rescued against his will by her footman, he found himself seated in the coach opposite her and two of her daughters. There he sulked until delivered back to his father's door and into the arms of his mother, who was advised by Lady Grange to keep her son nearer home.

It is possible that the mother was no more grateful for unsolicited advice on how to look after her son than the son was to be needlessly rescued. But despite his sulky behaviour, Alexander seems to have caught the interest of Jean and Rachel, the two girls in the coach. Soon afterwards they came to the manse accompanied by their younger brother, John, to invite Alexander to visit Preston House and drink tea with them. Carlyle's description of this juvenile tea-party is recalled in such detail that it must have been a high point in his childhood. It also provides a valuable cameo of the less-than-happy home life of the Granges.

The girls had a fine closet in which to hold their tea-party, furnished with chairs, a table, and a set of china. They had set about making the tea, with the help of a maid, when they were interrupted by the shrill voice of Lady Grange screaming 'Mary Erskine, my angel Mary Erskine'. The effect of this was dramatic. Both the girls and the maid seemed to be frightened out of their wits and even when the noise ceased the girls ordered John and Alexander to stand sentry, to give them advance warning if their mother should return. Alexander found that he was relieved when his father's man came to collect him at seven o'clock.

'I had no great enjoyment,' he writes, 'notwithstanding the good things and the kisses given, for I had by contagion caught a mighty fear of my lady from them. When I read the fable of the City Mouse and the Country Mouse this scene came fresh to my memory. What trials and dangers have children to go through.'

Even so, he managed to recover sufficiently once out of sight of the house and out of earshot of Lady Grange to open up the party bag of sweet cake, almonds, and raisins he had been given for his brother Loudwick, and deal with the contents. He had obviously omitted to tell his hostesses that Loudwick was no longer at home. In fact poor Loudwick had 'gone to die' at his grandfather's manse in Dumfriesshire, a piece of information Carlyle records matter-of-factly, mortal illness being one of the trials and dangers endured by children.

Carlyle's account of his visit to Preston House reads convincingly, and the timing is so significant. In less than two years the Granges would be living apart, and in less than three Lady Grange would with clinical efficiency be excised from all that she knew and reigned over. The calm acceptance by the family of their mother's disappearance would persuade many that it need not be a matter of concern to them either. If the family were not disturbed, then surely nothing sinister could have occurred?

By the time of Lady Grange's abduction Charles and James, the two eldest sons, were 22 and 19 years old respectively, adult enough to have at least made their objections known. Mary, the eldest daughter, was by then the Countess of Kintore, her ante-nuptial contract dated 21 August 1729, when she was barely 15. She had married well, much to the satisfaction of her mother. Yet no hue and cry was ever raised on behalf of Lady Grange by the daughter she had called her angel.

Carlyle's father, as the local minister, was much more involved than his son in the family at Preston House. In particular he was called upon to satisfy Lord Grange's appetite for religious disputation. As Lord Grange was a most important member of his congregation, it would have been unwise to refuse the invitation even if he had wished to do so. And so it fell that very frequently the minister found himself detained into the wee small hours in Grange's library, the understanding being that much of the time was spent in prayer and in settling high points of Calvinism. But Carlyle's mother suspected (and her suspicion somehow conveyed itself to her son) that the claret flowed freely.

Grange's library was situated within a pavilion of the house which extended out to a small wilderness of half an acre. This area was exclusively used by Lord Grange for meditation and prayer. Or so his admirers said. But the wilderness also had a secret door leading out to the fields beyond, which fuelled rumour that he sometimes played host to more than the local minister in his library and that fair maidens were also admitted.

More worrying to Lady Grange than her husband's possible philandering was the probability that Preston House was being used as a meeting place for those with a interest in Jacobitism and the restoration of the Stuarts to the British throne. Such treasonable activities were much more dangerous, and threatened her own social position as well as the wellbeing of her family. Mistresses and sexual peccadilloes might be overlooked, but the suspicion that her husband was imperilling the family's fortunes by contact with the deposed House of Stuart rang alarm bells. The catastrophic consequences of that were already writ large in the melancholy situation of James's brother.

Lady Grange was a woman who liked to be in command. Carlyle tells us that Grange had made her factor on his estate and given her the management of his affairs. When he was away from home he wrote her the most flattering letters and when present he 'imparted secrets' to her which, if disclosed, might have endangered his life. Carlyle also tells us that news of the London mistress, when it percolated back to Preston, 'did not tend to make the lady's behaviour less outrageous'.

Lady Grange was becoming increasingly incensed by her husband's sexual and political dalliances. Could she put a stop to the one by threatening to blow the whistle on the other? If hard evidence of a damaging nature to Grange and his friends should happen to fall into the hands of his wronged wife, how would she react? The contemporary playwright William Congreve had the answer, framed in a couplet which had become a popular quotation:

> Heav'n has no rage, like love to hatred turn'd
> Nor Hell a fury, like a woman scorn'd.

CHAPTER 7

Too Many Tears

*What was a man to do with such a wife? These were things which could not be
redressed in a court of justice, and we had not then a madhouse.*
Memorial to the arbitrators in the separation case, Lord Grange

THERE IS NO doubt that the good ship *Married Bliss*, crewed by James
and Rachel Erskine, had entered very choppy waters by 1730. In fact
it was badly holed, listing dangerously, and attracting a great deal of
attention. Relatives of both parties got together to discuss what might
be done in the way of a salvage operation in the best interests of all
concerned. Other more powerful, more shadowy figures, watched
intently from afar. They had no intention of allowing the foundering of
the Grange marriage to bring them down along with that particular leaky
vessel. Lives could be at risk if matters were not handled carefully.

It was essential to James that Rachel's unacceptable behaviour
towards himself and the children should be regarded as the sole reason
for the breakdown of his marriage. He was remarkably successful in
achieving this. Nobody seems to have raised the subject of his lordship's
marital infidelities, or thought fit to refer to late-night carousals at
Preston. And naturally there was no mention of any possible treasonable
activities. Lord Grange was above reproach, both as a family man and
as a loyal supporter of the Hanoverians, who had been seated, more or
less comfortably, on the British throne for the past 15 years.

Letters flew between family and friends in the spring of 1730 as Lady
Grange's behaviour became increasingly unpredictable. Her husband's
removal from her control of the factorship of his estate upset her greatly.
The decision was taken in absentia, from the safe distance of London.

Lady Grange became even more enraged when she discovered that the lock to the door of her husband's study had been changed without her knowledge. This had been done to ensure she could not gain access to the cabinet in which he kept papers now considered unwise for her to see. In a letter to his father, Charles reports his mother's fury when she learned of the locked door, 'speaking of it till she was hoarse'. Sir Hugh Paterson of Bannockburn, who was married to Grange's sister Jean, had been given the unenviable task of telling Rachel of the changed locks. 'Sir Hugh will have written. I know nothing of the conversation,' younger son James writes to Grange. 'Only when he came out from a certain person he was trembling like one in the fit of ane ague.'

It does seem grossly self-serving that at this juncture Lord Grange should leave his family and friends to cope with the situation at Preston. Near relatives, including Sir Hugh and David Erskine, Lord Dun, who was a fellow judge and close friend as well as a kinsman, were roped in to try and deal with his wife. The task proved beyond them. 'All of us are greatly difficulted, what part to act or what advice to give,' Lord Dun informs Grange in a letter dated 12 March 1730. Significantly he passes on the advice of others that Grange may have to tell his wife that 'you are resolved never to see her and that tho you've borne her violence you find it now impossible to bear it any longer for self-preservation and the good of your family and children'. For the first time the suggestion is being made that Grange might have to consider a legal separation.

The sons' letters make poignant reading. Emotional family scenes, and some hard home truths for Lord Grange to take on board, are all there. Like so many children of a failing marriage in any era, they find themselves caught up in the parental cross-fire.

Charles addresses his father as 'My Lord'. He is 20 years old and in his final letter has good news to report: his longed-for commission has finally come through. Charles would dearly have liked his commission to be the only thing of moment in his life. He can't wait to escape the problems of his dysfunctional family. James, aged 17, addresses his father as 'Dear Papa'. Often he is writing at the request of his mother, and to her dictation. His letters are full of details of her ill health and her chronic shortage of money. In one he comments, 'If any could do Mama good it is hearing that you are to be so short a time at London.'

Both sons mention the unmentionable. Charles tells his father that his mother 'spoke of Mrs Lindsey' when she read Lord Grange's letter stating that his business affairs would not allow him to leave London. James reports that she discusses her marital problems with the servants, and has told them that he would not allow her to come up to London 'where it was said you kept a whore'. Small wonder that James finishes off that particular letter with, 'My dear Papa, I beg ten thousand pardons for writing after this manner.' His writing deteriorates in later letters. He is obviously under great emotional strain. 'I could better bear her scolding than her weeping,' he comments at one point. Meanwhile Charles has been trying the soft approach to calm his mother. 'I believe you'll agree with me in thinking that when gentle means can be of use they are to be chosen rather than others,' he suggests to his father. But Lady Grange continues to rant and rave, to weep and threaten, to say one thing one day and contradict it the next: determine to go to London, then agree to wait till the roads are better; make plans to take the cure at Bath, having earlier declared she 'did not give a Farthing for Bath'.

Matters came to a head on 23 April when the family were staying in their townhouse. Charles was awakened by shrieks and cries, which at first he thought came from the nearby Cowgate. But it was his mother, crying, 'Murder, murder', threatening to run naked out into the street or to kill herself by throwing herself out of the window. James and Jean were also awakened and Lady Grange had to be put back to bed ranting against their father and his friends three times.

Charles confesses when he writes to tell his father of the night's 'alarums' that he would have let his mother do what she had threatened if she had got out of bed a fourth time. Perhaps he felt that the family could not be disgraced further, for he adds: 'It's talked through the town that my Lord Grange is a cruel man to leave his Lady to starve, with not wherewithall to buy her own or children's dinner.' In the end the sympathy of the older children for their mother ran out. To read their letters is to begin to understand why less than two years later she could be abducted into exile without any protest from her children. Meanwhile Grange was successfully presenting himself as a man much to be pitied. As proof of the stress of living with his volatile partner, he

David Erskine, Lord Dun (1670–1758).
Lawyer, kinsman and close friend of Lord Grange. Portrait by William Aikman.

produced the razor which she allegedly kept under her pillow. Friends were suitably shocked and passed the story on. One fervent admirer, the Reverend Robert Wodrow of Eastwood, rushed to his hero's defence, asserting in his *Analecta* that even Grange's enemies would admit that he had suffered the greatest provocations possible. In the public sympathy stakes as well as within the circle of her own family Rachel was losing the contest. Even her sister and brother-in-law, the Hamiltons of Olivestob, her near neighbours at Preston, and her kinsman Thomas Hope of Rankeillour, who would represent her interests in discussions over a possible legal separation, were persuaded that her behaviour was harming her family. On 27 July 1730 Rachel put her signature to a submissive letter of separation addressed to James Erskine of Grange.

My Dear – Since you are angry with me & will not live with me I promise that if you'l allow me a hundred pounds Str: yearly and pay it at two Terms in the year, in full of all I can ask or crave of you during the time I retire, and if you'l drop the Process of Separation you have raised against me befor the Commissars of Edinburgh then I will retire and live by my self for five years from the date hereof and shall not trouble you nor sett my Foot within your Doors in Town or Country and I also expect you'l [give] me such Household furniture Linnings and Plate as you think fitt for my service and use & I will instantly on your acceptance hereof retire from your House and fulfill what is above on Honour. Thes Letter I have writt and subscribed with my own hand at Edinburgh the twentyseven day of July one thousand seven hunder & thirty years.

I am, Your
Unfortunate tho obediente Wife
Rachell Erskine

CHAPTER 8

Separation

...we are in possession of no imputations against Lord Grange, which may
not be referred to or palliated by the maniac violence of his wife; and that,
while his public character was unreproached, hers was notorious for an
infamy of manners, which insulted and outraged all with whom she had
any correspondence, from humble menials to persons of the highest rank
scandalizing the town and alienating all her friends.
Tales of the Century, the Sobieski Stuarts

MARITAL MISERY WAS no less common in the 18th century than in the
present day but the moral climate of the time, combined with ignorance
of the law and limited access to it, ensured that most couples whom
God had joined together stayed that way for life. Yet Scots law did
provide a way out of a failed marriage for both men and women, even
if few took advantage of it. The problem for Lady Grange was that
her preferred option was no longer available to her. She still hoped for
a reconciliation with her husband. Even when she railed against him,
a letter from London could cause her to change her tone. She always
preferred to blame his friends. What she really wanted was for her
husband to come to heel, to abandon his London mistress, to restore
her position as his wife, to reinstate her as factor of the family estate
and to desist from any dangerous involvements with those of a Jacobite
persuasion. Quite a wish list, but the time was long past when Lord
Grange would have been willing to satisfy her on any of it.

She could have taken her husband to court for maintenance, as
her mother had done with her father. She could have raised an action
against him for adultery but she did neither of these things. Both were
cumbersome procedures and success was not assured. Instead she had

been persuaded by family and friends to accept a separation agreement conditional on Lord Grange dropping the formal application for separation which he had lodged with the courts. This he appears to have done, as there is no reference to the Grange case to be found in court registers. Even so, the separation document seems to have been legally binding and neither party was free to remarry. Although Lady Grange disappeared from Edinburgh society in January 1732 (and a rumour went around that she had died) Lord Grange did not marry Fanny Lindsay until he received confirmation of his wife's death in 1745.

As for the one hundred pounds alimony, it is impossible to determine how often she received it. However it is likely that Lord Grange provided money to the succession of Highland jailers – hardly the use she would have envisaged for her alimony when she signed that document in 1730. If indeed she did sign it. In her second letter from St Kilda she claims that, despite pressure from all sides, she had 'absolutely refused to subscribe to it' because she still loved her husband and separation was contrary to the vows she had taken before God. Yet comparison of her signature on the separation document with the one on her St Kilda letters would seem to indicate that in making this assertion she was being economical with the truth. But whether or not Lady Grange signed the separation document, it is clear she gave, at the very least, tacit consent.

Before long she began to break her side of the bargain. Even though she had agreed to distance herself from her family, she moved to Edinburgh, taking a room near the family home, 'that I might have the pleasure to see the house he was in and see him and my children when going in and out', as she explains in her second St Kilda letter, in which she further admits that she did not leave her husband alone but instead approached people, including advocates and ministers, to try and persuade him of the sin he had committed by 'putting away' his wife 'contrary to the laws of God and man'. Both were devout Christians, so this was the most powerful argument in her armoury.

The picture drawn by Lady Grange of herself as a mother desperate for a sight of her children would have gained her little contemporary sympathy. In those days courts commonly awarded custody of children

Sir Hugh Paterson of Bannockburn, MP for Stirlingshire, husband of Lord Grange's sister Jean, and stalwart family friend. Painted by David Allan.

to the husband, who, as head of the family, was considered responsible for their upbringing and education. Exceptions were made only in cases of extreme brutality by the father or because of the extreme youth of the children. It is practically inconceivable that Lady Grange would have been given custody even if she had enjoyed a close, happy relationship with her children. That this was not the case is supported by Carlyle's

LADY JANE PATTERSON, Wife of SIR HUGH PATTERSON.
D.ʳ of CHARLES 5.ᵗʰ EARL of MAR, Died 1765
By DAVID ALLAN.

Lady Jean Paterson, who was given the care of the younger Grange children after Lord and Lady Grange separated. Painted by David Allan.

description of family life at Preston. After the separation Lord Grange moved the family into his townhouse in Niddry's Wynd with his sister, Lady Jean Paterson, now acting as housekeeper and substitute mother. An indication of Lady Grange's response to this arrangement is to be found in *Tales of the Century* by the Sobieski Stuarts, according to whom the two women met in Merlin's Wynd, one of the oldest streets in Edinburgh, which now lies under the city's Tron Church. Lady Jean was accompanied by young Jean, Lady Grange's daughter. 'Come away from that slut, your aunt,' Lady Grange is supposed to have said, 'for you are my own dear bairn, and sharp and smart like myself, and will not be a tawpie like her.' The 'dear bairn', not surprisingly, burst into tears. Lady Grange is further accused of accosting her husband in the street and attempting to disturb him in church when the minister was in the pulpit. On one occasion, when Grange emerged with one of the children she pursued them through the crowd which had gathered, 'raising so great a clamour that they were compelled to take refuge in a tavern in the Writers' Court where she imprisoned them for more than two hours, by waiting for their reappearance at the head of the close.' The Sobieski Stuarts may exaggerate but other contemporary reports suggest that the famous Chiesley temper was providing ammunition for her detractors.

Lord Grange never forgot this public humiliation. When letters from his wife finally reached Edinburgh some ten years later detailing her abduction and imprisonment, Thomas Hope wrote to him seeking an explanation. Grange's response reeks of self-justification: 'I beginn my answer by putting you in mind of certain facts, which ye cannot hav forgot,' he opens, before launching into a catalogue of his wife's transgressions – 'attacking the house, cursing the children, crying and raging [at him] in the streets and among the footmen and chairmen of visitors'. She threatened to denounce him while sitting in judgment on the bench, 'which dreading she would do every time I went to it, made my duty there very heavy on me, least that honourable Court of Session should have been disturbed and affronted on my occasion.'

CHAPTER 9

The Loose Cannon

We have no real concept today what it was like to be a Jacobite then,
when that name incurred the peril of the gibbet and the axe. Few of those
astonished at the banishment of Lady Grange comprehend the danger of her
husband and friends, when one word from a desperate woman should have
perilled the best heads in Scotland.
Tales of the Century, the Sobieski Stuarts

What effect her lies may have... one cannot certainly know; but if proper
measures be not fallen against it, the creature may prove troublesome.
Lord Grange to Thomas Erskine of Pittodry, 22 March 1731

ROBERT WODROW, A staunch supporter of Lord Grange, hints in his
contemporary notes at the hidden agenda behind the vilification of Lady
Grange, while being careful to dismiss any accusations of treason made
by her as entirely without foundation. Writing of the open break in the
marriage, he claims that she set spies on her husband in London and
intercepted his letters at the Post Office. Some of the letters, intended for
Lord Dun, she had taken in the summer of 1730 to the Justice Clerk in
Edinburgh, on the grounds that they were treasonable and that certain
phrases related to the Pretender. Wodrow dismisses this interpretation
as being 'without the least shaddou for the inference'.

The following spring Lord Grange offloaded his concerns about the
situation in a rambling letter to Thomas Erskine of Pittodry. One of
his main objects might have been to touch his cousin for money (or
at least make Thomas aware of his impecunious state), for he pleads
poverty and bemoans the demands being made upon him as the sole
defender of the interest of the Mar estates. The letter is revealing as to

his state of mind at this vital period, while Rachel is still unconstrained in Edinburgh. He is obviously jumpy, mentioning risks being run which could lead to execution on London's Tyburn or in Edinburgh's Grass Market. He advises Thomas to keep this letter for his own eyes only and to burn it without delay – advice which was evidently ignored. From this letter, it would seem that the old-boy network is holding firm. The Lord Justice Clerk when he hears of Lady Grange's intention to come to him with accusations of high treason backed up with signed information, instructs his footman, if the 'mad woman' should appear, to turn her down stairs.

London is more difficult. Grange has never lacked enemies in that city, has always been regarded with suspicion by some who have long memories of his brother's treason. The main problem there is the situation of his sister-in-law, Frances Pierrepoint, Lady Mar, the second wife of his exiled brother, who has been declared 'lunatick' and is in London in the care of her sister, the redoubtable Lady Mary Wortley Montagu. There is little love lost between Lord Grange and Lady Mary. Grange expands at great length on the difficulties he has with Lady Mary.

Lady Mar is now quite well, he informs Thomas. She should no longer be detained as a lunatic, but is obstinately averse to appearing in chancery to have the detention order removed. Grange suspects this is the work of Lady Mary who would lose not only the custody of her sister but also the £500 which she gets yearly from the Mar estates, if the order were to be lifted.

Then there is the added complication of a house in Whitehall which had been granted to Lady Mar by the king and which is currently leased to Lord Grange. Grange has now got a new lease from the king and has already sold both leases for £1,670 to help pay off Mar debts in Paris. But if Lady Mar stays under the control of her sister she probably won't ratify the arrangement of the lease, and if his brother, who is in poor health, should die (as indeed he does a year later, still in exile in Aachen) then Mar's only daughter might also fall into the clutches of Lady Mary which would 'go near to finish the ruine of the family'. He adds to all this prophecy of doom the fact that the financial resources of the Mar estates are vastly low. Grange tells Thomas that he has taken

John Erskine, 6th Earl of Mar, before forfeiture of the earldom, with his only son, Thomas, holding a parrot. Painted by Sir Godfrey Kneller c.1715.

nothing from his brother for all the legal costs he has incurred, and that when he goes south he is quite abstemious. He has even lost his relish for French claret, the most expensive article to be had in the southern capital.

In 1724 the forfeited Mar estates, thanks to the efforts of Lord Grange and Lord Dun, had been purchased and brought back into family ownership. But the foreign debts incurred by the exiled earl and the duty James Erskine considered was his to press for his brother's pardon, plus the perceived indolence of Mar's son and heir, Lord Erskine, (who was more inclined to spend time on his flute and on tennis than on family matters), plus the interference of Lady Mary as self-appointed champion of her sister and her sister's only child, Lady Frances Erskine, all combined to occupy Lord Grange's attention and make his life something of a misery. No wonder he felt the need to unburden himself to a sympathetic fellow Erskine.

Grange is now having to consider the necessity of going to London again as he has had letters from two of Lady Mar's closest friends entreating him to see what he can do to help her. He will go, he assures his cousin, though his health the past winter has not been good, and he will require to make the journey by 'easy posting'. He does not think the matter of Lady Mar will be easy to solve – no help is to be expected from previous friends who are now keeping their distance in case 'their own fingers should be burnt'. Grange does not enlarge on why this should be so but perhaps these previous friends have heard something of Lady Grange's antics in Edinburgh.

There is some dubiety about the precise content of the intercepted papers mentioned by Wodrow as now being in Lady Grange's possession. They may have contained only an account of Grange's past proceedings in the matter of his sister-in-law, Lady Mar. Since Walpole, the de facto prime minister of the time, is supposed to have treated Lady Mar badly, that could mean the papers also included some ill-judged remarks by Grange about Walpole. Political suicide perhaps, but scarcely a hanging matter.

However there is also a possibility – the Sobieski Stuarts describe it as a distinct possibility – that the papers also contained 'dangerous communications relative to the house of Stuart', linked to the names of

Frances Pierrepoint (1690–1761), second wife of the 6th Earl of Mar, with her only daughter, Frances, at a harpsichord. Painted by Francesco Trevisani c.1719, when the family were at the Jacobite court in Rome.

such distinguished personages in Scotland as Sir Alexander Macdonald of Sleat, Lord Lovat, and Norman MacLeod of Dunvegan. A much more serious business altogether.

If Lady Grange's accusations can be confined to Scotland it should still be possible to keep a lid on the business. Many distinguished families in both Scotland and England are still hedging their bets at this time on the possibility of a Jacobite restoration, but they are careful what they commit to paper. If Lord Grange has been indiscreet then more decisive action may have to be taken to deal with the situation.

So Lord Grange goes south in the spring of 1731, intent on wresting his sister-in-law out of the expensive care of Lady Mary. He confides to his cousin that he might even attempt to take Lady Mar over to her exiled husband. The dangers of going across to see his brother would be eased if he is escorting his brother's wife, but he can't judge how this will go till he gets to London. All will depend on how he finds men's faces and dispositions towards him.

Alas for such ambitious plans. A second letter to Thomas Erskine of 14 June 1731 carries the news that Lord Grange has been bested by Lady Mary over the custody of Lady Mar. Nonetheless the incorrigible James Erskine is not downhearted; he takes as his text Ecclesiastes, Chapter 5, Verse 8: 'If thou seest the oppression of the poor, and violent perverting of judgment and justice in a province, marvel not at the matter: for he that is higher than the highest regardeth and there be higher than they.' In other words Grange is sure the Almighty is on his side.

'I thank God I have never yet found myself inclined to be discouraged by any disappointments or difficultys as to despond, or like men in a sinking ship to quit helm and tackle, and wait their fate without working,' he assures Thomas. 'My philosophy in that case is this. Everyone cannot have always a good hand deallt out to him at cards, nor an easy or prosperous part alloted to him in a tragedy or comedy; but he does well who plays his hand and acts the part right, whatever it be.' The problem is that he has no control over the part that might be played by his wife.

Grange knows that if Rachel goes to London she will attempt to gain access to Lady Mary. He has already confided to his cousin that Lady

John Erskine, 6th Earl of Mar (1675–1732) in exile, wearing both the Thistle from Queen Anne and the Garter from James III. Painting c.1719 attributed to Francesco Trevisani

Grange 'openly blesses Lady Mary for her opposition to our friends'. On a personal level the two ladies have a grievance in common. Lady Mary's contention, repeated loudly and as often as opportunity allows to Lord Grange himself, is that her sister has been driven mad by her husband's bad usage. Rachel is likely to recognise a parallel there to her own situation with the husband's brother.

In her letters from St Kilda Lady Grange claims that her first inclination after the breakdown of her marriage was to go to London. However she postponed that decision, preferring to move into a chamber in a private house in Edinburgh, in the hope that Lord Grange would alter his temper. When it became obvious that this was not going to happen she resolved to go to London, to live with some of her friends there and make herself as easy as she could without him.

Consequently in January 1732 Lady Grange booked and paid part in advance for a seat on the stagecoach which departed regularly at that time from the Canongate in Edinburgh for the metropolis. Almost immediately, according to the Sobieski Stuarts, the managers of the stage received a visit from a gentleman of considerable figure and fortune with interests in their business, who leaned with immediate effect on them. The hire fare already paid by Lady Grange was returned and her place given to another. The loose cannon had become too dangerous. London certainly was out and Edinburgh might well be becoming so. Harder men than Lord Grange had entered into the equation.

Quickly the matter was resolved and Lady Grange's fate sealed. She would be removed to a location far from the ken of most Lowland Scots, to a place where the inhabitants spoke a different language and were loyal only to the interests of their clan chiefs. Any damaging allegations Lady Grange might make would fall on deaf ears, or be muffled into silence by her distance from those who might give them credence.

CHAPTER 10

The *Enlèvement*

...upon the 22d of Jan 1732 I lodged in Margaret McLean's house and a
little before twelve at night Mrs McLean being on the plot opened the door
and there rush'd in to my room some servants of Lovats and his Couson
Roderick MacLeod he is a writter to the Signet they threw me down upon
the floor in a Barbarous manner I cri'd murther murther then they stopp'd
my mouth I puled out the cloth and told Rod:MacLeod I knew him their
hard rude hands bleed and abassed my face all below my eyes they dung out
some of my teeth and toere the cloth of my head and toere out some of my
hair I wrestled and defend'd my self with my hands then Rod: order'd to
tye down my hands and cover my face most pityfully there was no skin left
on my face with a cloath and stopp'd my mouth again they had wrestl'd so
long with me that it was all that I could breath, then they carry'd me down
stairs as a corps at the stair-foot they had a Chair and Alexander Foster of
Carsboony in the Chair who took me on his knee I made all the struggel I
could but he held me fast in his arms my mouth being stopp'd I could not
cry they carr'd me off very quickly without the Port...
Lady Grange's letter from St Kilda, 20 January 1738

ONCE THE DECISION had been taken to remove Lady Grange from
Edinburgh it was acted upon without delay. Within two days of the
cancelled coach booking Rachel had late-night visitors to her lodgings.
It was too late for a social call, but the men said they had an important
letter and message to deliver and were admitted.

The midnight callers were two Highland gentlemen, Macdonald of
Morar and MacLeod of Berneray, accompanied by servants. Their message was that, at the behest of her husband, they were to convey her to
a place of security in the country. It was obvious that a polite refusal
was not going to be an acceptable response. Lady Grange did not leave

quietly. As her own account graphically bears witness, the struggle in Mrs McLean's best room was brutal and bloody. Yet no one came to her aid. The servants had either been sent to bed early or despatched on errands. The role of Mrs McLean, the landlady, remains obscure. The most likely explanation of Lady Grange's lonely ordeal was the disinclination of the lower orders to become involved in a matter which obviously involved personages of power and influence.

Lady Grange put up a good fight but superior strength prevailed. She was bundled into a sedan chair already occupied by Alexander Foster of Carsbonny, a man she would come to know well. Swiftly she was carried away through the north port of the town, never again to set foot in Edinburgh.

On the ridge of a hill in the open countryside beyond the town a silent group of six or seven men with horses awaited the arrival of the kidnappers. Lady Grange was quickly transferred from chair to horseback and tied securely to Foster to prevent any possible escape attempt. The men already knew the defiant spirit of their captive.

It was a bitterly cold night with little cloud cover. Lady Grange appealed for some respite, showing them the bloody linen cloths which covered her wounds. But her captors were men under orders, who knew that to be discovered in this risky undertaking could endanger their own lives. Their response was as hard and chill as the night itself. Without delay the party moved off, keen to put as much distance as possible between themselves and the scene of the crime.

Despite all she had recently gone through Lady Grange kept her wits about her and years later she would name names and record her ordeal in detail. Although Foster told her the men were his servants, she was sure that this was not true and that some of them were the servants of Lovat, chief of the Clan Fraser. She was aware that they were heading west towards the Linlithgow road by the 'Lang Gait', a track roughly following the line of present-day Princes Street. The transfer to horseback, according to Lady Grange, had taken place at Mutter's, or Multer's, Hill. This appears as Muletrees Hill on John Laurie's 1763 map of Edinburgh and is commemorated today by a side-lane in the fashionable shopping area of St Andrew Square. As the party travelled the Lang Gait that cold January night in 1732, Edinburgh slept snug

Lady Grange's Edinburgh. Hollar's 1670 view.

behind its walls and ports, the moonlight glancing on the waters of the Nor' Loch which for so long had formed part of the town's northern boundary.

Yet all of this before long was going to change dramatically. In 1752 plans would be approved which would lead to the draining of the Nor' Loch, its replacement by public gardens, and the building of new streets and houses on the very land which Lady Grange's party were presently traversing. In the 1760s the first elegant Georgian houses would go up to the south of the town with the building of George Square, to be followed later by the massive expansion to the north and the creation of the New Town. As the upper classes moved out, the social mix in the crowded squalor of Lady Grange's Edinburgh would become only a memory, a past chapter in the town's history.

It seems to have been Lady Grange's fate always to be on the cusp of great changes, but not to live long enough to benefit from them. The Edinburgh she was leaving behind would change within the lifetime of some of her younger companions. The place to which she was going, though she did not know it yet, was the Gaelic west, still ruled by its clan chiefs and still largely unknown to the rest of Scotland. Yet this too would change with the crushing of the Second Jacobite Rising in 1746, the building of new roads, and the absorption of the *Gàidhealtachd* into the British state. The prison which was able to enclose her so completely in the 1730s would be split open after the defeat of the Highland clans at Culloden.

As she passed the massive bulk of the Castle Rock and prepared to leave Edinburgh behind, did some sixth sense persuade Lady Grange to twist round for a last look back at the town she would never see again? Or was she mercifully unaware of the finality of the fate that had been decreed for her by her husband and his powerful friends?

Before long Lady Grange began to complain of a stitch in her side due to her constrained position on the horse, and appealed to Foster to allow her to alight. Foster's response was to have the gag replaced in her mouth, calling her a damned bitch and threatening to break her neck if she did not hold her peace. Was he not, he reminded her, venturing his life for her? There is only her word for this incident, but it is not difficult to believe. The enterprise was fraught with danger and the kidnappers were, as she later described them, 'always in terrour'. If she cried out, if questions were asked, the whole undertaking might founder.

Twenty miles of night-riding brought the party to Muiravonside, just beyond Linlithgow, the home of the advocate John MacLeod. The conspirators had rightly calculated that by travelling at night and at the weekend there was less likelihood of others being on the road. By daybreak they were at their destination, having met no one.

Servants with torches showed the reluctant guest to a comfortable bedchamber with a fire and good linen marked – as the sharp-eyed Lady Grange did not fail to note – with John MacLeod's name. There was to be no rest, however, for the lady. She could not even divest herself of her clothes, since Sandy Fraser, one of Lovat's servants, was detailed to stay with her constantly. By the following nightfall the party was preparing to move on again. Lady Grange refused to co-operate and had to be carried downstairs by Fraser and put on the horse once more with Foster. It was now the Sabbath, when few people would be travelling, and they avoided the substantial town of Falkirk by taking a route through the Torwood. Lady Grange recognised the area: she had been that way before, perhaps on a visit in happier times to her mother-in-law when she was resident at Stirling Castle.

They were now approaching Wester Pomais. Its tower dungeon would be her prison until 15 August, when she would finally be transported across to the west coast of Scotland and out to the islands. If there was to be any chance of rescue it would have to be at Pomais, before she was taken beyond contact with people and places she knew.

Meanwhile back in Edinburgh, Lord Grange was coping with enquiries as to the sudden disappearance of his wife. Some of his friends would know the whole story, some would know only a sanitised version, and some would know nothing at all. Some were persuaded to believe that Lady Grange had died. There is a lingering tradition that a funeral for Lady Grange took place at Greyfriars. If this funeral did happen, it would be only the first of several. A second took place at Duirinish churchyard at Dunvegan in Skye in 1745, when many people were invited to attend the burial of the strange lady who had come to live among them. The coffin was filled with sods of earth. The real burial took place secretly several miles away at Trumpan in Waternish.

When the Reverend Archibald Clerk, minister in the parish of Duirinish in Skye, came to write the report on his parish for *The New Statistical Account of Scotland* in 1845, he recalled the two funerals in Skye for Lady Grange, adding, 'There are few people who have had so many funerals as Lady Grange and few also who have had more cause to long for a real one.'

CHAPTER II

Wester Pomais

[Foster] took me to the house of Pomeis thro a vault to a low room all the
windows nailed up with thick board and no light in the room he was so cruel
as to leave me all aloan and two doors lock'd on me
Letter from St Kilda, 20 January 1738, Lady Grange

WESTER POMAIS WAS owned by a Mr Stewart, a man with Jacobite
sympathies. Alexander Foster was employed there as his factor and
it was his responsibility to arrange the purchase of all necessary
provisions for Lady Grange, including such things as coal and candles.
These were then delivered to her by Andrew Leishman, the tenant at
Wester Pomais. His wife was on hand to attend to her personal needs, a
striking reminder that a lady was still considered to be a lady, however
reduced her circumstances – even one who had been so roughly handled
that she was now missing at least two of her teeth, as well as some of
her hair.

The lodgings in which Lady Grange now found herself were a
sore come-down from what she had been used to at Preston House.
Pomais Tower had been uninhabited for some time and the windows
of her room were boarded-up. Locked in the ground floor of the tower
behind two doors secured with cross-bars, she passed most of her time
in semi-darkness. The only source of light came from a shot-hole in an
adjoining closet. The furniture consisted of a very old ugly bed without
a 'roof' and a timber chair with only half a bottom to it.

Her complaints that her health was being affected by lack of
fresh air and exercise were unlikely to have been met with sympathy
from Foster, who had kept his distance since their arrival at Pomais.

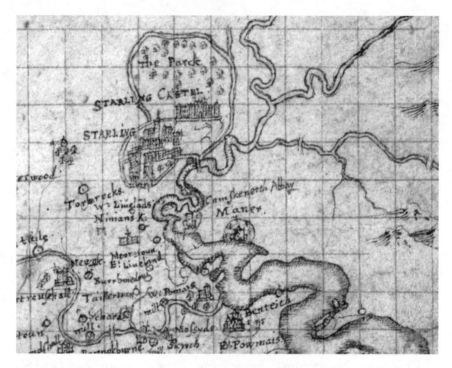

A section of Timothy Pont's 16th-century map of the East Central Lowlands. Wester Pomais tower, where Lady Grange was held prisoner in 1732, is shown south of 'Starling' (Stirling), near the winding River Forth.

Leishman proved more malleable. Perhaps influenced by his wife, he was so disturbed by the conditions in which Lady Grange was being kept that he told Foster he wished to have no hand in the lady's death. Foster then conceded Lady Grange access to the upper chambers of the tower and to the enclosed courtyard, under the supervision of James Fraser, who had stayed on to act as a guard.

There were considerable comings and goings at Pomais, for the Leishmans, and George Ross the resident gardener and his wife Agnes, had grown-up families who visited their parents regularly. Ross also owned a meal yard and house in nearby Stirling. Lady Grange did her best to capitalise on the situation. Although she was deprived of writing materials she claims that she managed to give 'some thing' to the two sons and a daughter of the gardener, in the hope that they might contact the ministers of Stirling, Hamilton, and Erskine, and tell them of her imprisonment. On another occasion she spoke to the Leishmans' son and three daughters when she saw them in the courtyard, informing them she was Lord Grange's wife, 'in hopes they would lett it be knowen'. It was all to no avail. Lady Grange was effectively sealed within a private fiefdom, her existence not to be acknowledged beyond the locked courtyard gate. Provisions brought for her use were explained away as being for the gardener and his wife. Those to whom she had personally appealed knew better than to meddle in the business of the powerful men who were involved in her imprisonment.

Winter turned to spring, spring to summer and still Lady Grange remained at Pomais. Lord Lovat passed through Stirling several times during this period, taking the opportunity to meet Foster and Fraser and receive reports on the prisoner. Was there a problem somewhere? Pomais was surely meant to be only a temporary holding post. Perhaps there was a difficulty with the sea transport to take Lady Grange from the mainland of Scotland out to the remote island already selected for her permanent, more easily managed imprisonment.

On 12 August, however, there was a new development. Peter Fraser, Lord Lovat's page, arrived at Pomais with three companions. Three days later, at ten at night, Foster entered the prisoner's room, accompanied by Peter and James Fraser and another Highlander called Alexander Grant, to inform her that she must come with them. When she put up resistance, she was carried bodily out of the house by the two Frasers and set on horseback. After almost seven months at Pomais, the next stage of the journey into exile had begun.

CHAPTER 12

Into the *Gàidhealtachd*

I was set on a horse behind that vil'd paest fellow James Fraser, I can not
write the anguish and sorrow I was in I never read or hear'd of any Wife
whatever was her crime so cruelly and barbarously treatt as I have been.
Letter from St Kilda, 20 January 1738 – Lady Grange

Lady Grange was still attempting to raise the alarm but it would not have
helped as the company were prepared to say she was an insane lady they
were conveying to or from St Fillan's Pool, according to the relation of their
route to that place.
Tales of the Century, the Sobieski Stuarts

THE BRIDGE AT Stirling, viewed in the moonlight by Lady Grange as she
was taken north, was to be her last glimpse of a recognisable world.
From then on she knew no more of the way. Even so, her accounts of the
journey, given in her two letters from St Kilda, are the best sources we
have to establish the approximate route of the party and to appreciate
the desperate nature of the enterprise.

From the moment she was forced onto horseback at Pomais on 15
August, until she was carried aboard a waiting sloop at Loch Hourn
on the north-west coast of Scotland on 10 September, she was the only
woman in the company of rough, uncommunicative men. But she had
yet to appreciate how radically her life had changed. Deference to her
social status now meant nothing compared to loyalty to the wishes of a
clan chief. If she expected anything better of Foster and Leishman, who
rode with the party for the first few days, or of Roderick MacLeod,
the Edinburgh lawyer with a love of Gaelic poetry who, with Lovat,
masterminded this part of the journey, then she was sorely disappointed.

Foster saw her into a room at the first halt, sat with her a little, and then 'never came near me after that'. She caught a glimpse of MacLeod at that first house but afterwards he too kept well out of her way. When Foster and Leishman took their departure, Lady Grange watched them ride off as she 'look't out at a hole' from the hut in which she had been confined. No final visit or final word of farewell, just as there had rarely been a kindly word before.

For the next part of the journey Alexander Grant was put in charge of her, riding behind her on the same horse. She dismisses him as a 'silly fellow' who had probably feigned his name. He was soon replaced by the much tougher James Fraser, Lord Lovat's footman, who had held the courtyard keys at Pomais and was more experienced in dealing with her. Much to her displeasure, she was tied to James. But the men knew that without such a restraint she would leap off the horse and attempt escape. Every time she was moved on, she never failed to tell her companions that they should consider what they were doing, reminding them that they were taking her away against her will. As if they needed any reminding.

The ill-assorted cavalcade at first travelled only by night, but as they penetrated further into the Highlands, where they felt they could trust the people, it was easier to negotiate the unmade roads and ford the rivers by daylight. Whenever possible they stayed in safe houses. More often they were forced to seek shelter in wretched inns, half-ruined buildings, byres or sheilings. On one occasion Lady Grange was simply laid down on the grass, where she slept, exhausted after a night of riding. How far distant the luxuries of Edinburgh and Preston must have seemed to her then.

The initial route north is fairly easy to determine. Lady Grange herself writes that she was brought into General Wade's new way, the road built after the Jacobite Rising of 1715 to link Perthshire with Fort William. Though this new road would make the journey easier, it brought its own dangers. It would have to be used sparingly and at night, when there were fewer people abroad. Skirting the settlements of Doune and Callander, the party progressed through Perthshire, and on to the MacGregor territory of Strathyre. From Balquhidder they crossed the moor to Glen Dochart and on again to Glencoe where Lady

Glencoe has a desolate reputation but Lady Grange is said to have spent her most agreeable night there on the journey north.

Grange apparently spent her most agreeable night. Her hosts treated her with kindness, oblivious to the reality of her situation, which she was unable to communicate to them since they had no English.

Lady Grange's passage through MacGregor country has inspired some stories in that clan's memoirs which may not have much basis in fact. Did she really traverse the narrow pass above the Falls of Leny by moonlight? The anonymous bearer of this particular tradition felt confident enough to claim that she would have enjoyed the sublimity of the scene, 'if only her spirits had been in their wonted elevations'. From the same source comes a colourful tale of the party falling into the hands of a robber band and being imprisoned in a half-ruinous castle in the vicinity of Balquidder, where they were hospitably entertained. In the great hall, hung with the skins and horns of wild beasts, rusty swords and old muskets, they were treated to a meal of venison supplied from a pot slung over the fire. Lady Grange is said to have slept on a heather bed covered with deerskins. Before the next day's departure, effected by a mix of force and bribery, she is supposed to have promised a large reward for her release. Clan MacLeod genealogy notes back up much of this story, claiming that Roderick MacLeod and Macdonald of Morar resorted to their dirks and pistols to escape after taking shelter in a robbers' hut (downgraded in this version from the MacGregors' castle). In the lawless Highlands of the first half of the 18th century, this incident might well have happened.

Lady Grange herself makes no mention of such adventures, but letters written so many years later and after such a variety of experiences could hardly have contained all she might have wished to chronicle on the limited amount of paper at her disposal. She makes no mention either of St Fillan's Pool, though this is one of the more believable tales told about the journey north. The waters of this deep natural pool located on a sharp bend of the River Fillan between Crianlarich and Tyndrum were thought to have been beneficial for those suffering mental illness. The unfortunates were plunged repeatedly into the pool before being tied up and left overnight in the nearby chapel, with St Fillan's Bell suspended over them. If they succeeded in untying themselves by morning, or had been miraculously unloosened, this was considered a good omen for their recovery.

Roderick MacLeod is credited with the idea of using a journey to or from the pool as a means to allay any concerns that might be aroused by the sight of an obviously distressed woman, bound, on horseback, being escorted by a band of men. It was the perfect cover. Lady Grange, with no knowledge of Gaelic, in an area where few spoke English, could neither contradict what was being said about her, nor make her true predicament known. She may not even have been aware of the subterfuge.

CHAPTER 13

Out to the Isles

...all the men being highlanders, none understood her clamours except the
master of the vessel.
Tales of the Century, the Sobieski Stuarts

THE REAL PUZZLE of the journey north is the route taken after leaving
Glencoe. Fort William, with its garrison of Government soldiers, would
surely have to be avoided. Yet both MacGregor and MacLeod sources
claim that Lady Grange was taken north to Loch Eil, just across the
water from the garrison town. According to these sources, she was then
taken by rowing boat to the head of Loch Eil, where she was placed
on horseback in an exhausted condition for the overland journey to
Glenfinnan. From there, another rowing boat took the party down Loch
Shiel and on to Castle Tioram, set on a small tidal island near the mouth
of Loch Moidart in the Ardnamurchan Peninsula. In 1715 the castle
had been set on fire by Allan, Chief of Clanranald, shortly before the
Battle of Sheriffmuir where he was killed fighting for the Old Pretender.
Since then the castle had lain unoccupied, but accommodation of a
kind would have been hastily arranged for the travellers. There would
have been little time for Lady Grange to recuperate at Castle Tioram,
for the necessity to get her off the Scottish mainland before the autumn
gales would have been uppermost in the minds of the kidnappers. They
were soon on the move again. A sloop awaited further north at Loch
Hourn. The journey, in a four-oared boat, is supposed to have taken a
day and a night.

Lady Grange's name is linked to Castle Tioram with the tenacity of
folk-tale. During her short stay there she is said to have tried to escape,

Castle Tioram in Moidart, seat of the Clanranalds, is said to have been a temporary prison for Lady Grange.

breaking her arm on the castle stairs on her way to a secret passage. In another version she attempts to escape through a narrow aperture in the castle wall, known to this day as 'the lady's hole'. Neither of these experiences are mentioned by Lady Grange. Perhaps, instead, she was held at the castle in 1741, when she had to be hurriedly removed from St Kilda and a grim game of hide and seek was played out in the Western Isles.

A much more likely route from Glencoe would have been to head north-east, giving Fort William a wide berth. Agreement had already been reached with the Macdonells of Glengarry to take charge of this next stage of the journey. A hand-over point somewhere on the north side of Loch Ness would have been the obvious choice.

The accounts of both Lady Grange and the Sobieski Stuarts support this. Even though she was handicapped by a lack of knowledge of Highland geography and by her unfamiliarity with Gaelic place-names, she is specific that on 28 August she arrived at Milltown, on Lord

Lovat's ground, where she was left with a reduced guard while the rest went on ahead, presumably to check the embarkation arrangements.

Milltown or *Baile-mhuileainn* was a common enough place-name. The Sobieski Stuarts pinpoint this particular Milltown as being in Stratherrick, on the south bank of Loch Ness, correcting Lady Grange's date for arrival there to 20 August, which fits in better with her own assertion that she remained there for 16 days, in dire need of rest: she had not slept in a bed since she left Pomais and one of her breasts had been hurt by the rough treatment she had received.

Around 5 September Alexander Grant returned with the rest of the guard. Lady Grange was taken by boat across an unnamed loch, which must surely have been Loch Ness. The Frasers, some of whom had been her constant companions since her abduction, now felt able to hand over their captive completely to the Macdonells, who proved equally determined jailers.

Ahead lay another tough leg of the journey, along the track through Glen Garry. By 10 September the party reached the agreed rendezvous at Loch Hourn and Lady Grange was carried on board the waiting sloop. The Sobieski Stuarts record, with a hint of sadistic satisfaction, that no one understood the prisoner's clamours. Master of the vessel Alexander Macdonald, the only English-speaker, was to be her host and jailer for approximately the next two years.

CHAPTER 14
Heskeir

I told him I was stolen out of Edinburgh, and brought there by force, and
that it was contrary to the laws what they were doing. He answered that
he could not keep me or any other against their will, except Sir Alexander
Macdonald were in the affair. How far Sir Alexander is concerned in this I
am not certain; but the man being poor and greedy of money, made him go
beyond his own light.
Letter from St Kilda, 21 January, 1741 – Lady Grange

IF LADY GRANGE had been unaware in her previous life of the way the
Gaelic world operated, she was by now having to come to terms with
its harsh reality. Clan loyalty was stronger than any rule of law, or any
inclination to question the actions of the chief. While the sloop waited
at Loch Hourn for a favourable wind she had several visitors, young
scions of the ruling clan of the area. 'They came with design to see
me, but not to relieve me,' she remembered bitterly. Yet there was one
visitor who might have helped her. William Toling a former merchant
in Inverness, had been in Edinburgh at the time of her disappearance.
He understood English and listened sympathetically to her tale of
misfortune, then promised to inform Thomas Hope, her lawyer, of
where she was to be taken.

Toling (or Tolmy) was a tenant on the lands of MacLeod. Perhaps he
had a subsequent visit from someone who re-arranged his priorities for
him, as had happened to the managers of the stagecoach in Edinburgh.
For whatever reason nothing came of his promise. There would be no
other offer of help for at least the next seven years.

Macdonald's sloop was 'storm-stay'd' for several days, finally leaving on 19 September. It soon ran into more stormy weather and, in

the opinion of Lady Grange at least, was almost shipwrecked before arriving at the Monach Islands eleven days later. A scattering of islets off the west coast of North Uist, the Monachs must have seemed an ideal choice for the confinement of the difficult, potentially dangerous Lady Grange. No one there was likely to listen to, or pass on, any information she might attempt to impart on the seditious activities of her husband and his friends.

Some perception of what awaited her there can be gleaned from Donald Monro's *A Description of the Occidental Islands of Scotland*. Monro was Archdeacon of the Western Isles in pre-Reformation Scotland and the book is thought to have been based on a tour he made of his spiritual territory some time around 1549. He is unlikely to have personally visited more than a fraction of the 250 islands listed in his book, relying instead on carefully collating information provided to him, but he may have gone to the Monachs since there was a religious settlement there.

The main island, then named Helsker na caillach, belonged in his time to the nuns of Colmkill, possibly a daughter-house of Columba's original foundation on Iona. Although Helsker was the largest island in the group it measured only about four miles by half a mile and possessed, according to Monro, good land for growing corn. The only other Monach island named by him is Haifsker, a rockier island noteworthy only for its regular seal culls.

By the time of Lady Grange's arrival, the Monachs belonged to Sir Alexander Macdonald of Sleat. The nuns had long gone, but the isolation of the islands which had attracted them there and the harsh environment which had challenged the strength of their vocation were still unchanged. Such conditions were hardly likely to have an equal appeal for an upper-class lady used to the sophistication of Edinburgh society, who only a short time before had been contemplating taking the waters at Bath and visiting friends in London. However, with no choice in the matter, Lady Grange came to live on Heskeir with Alexander Macdonald and his wife in the only decent habitation on the island. Alexander was tacksman to Sir Alexander, living a notch or two above the island's wretched cottars from whom he collected rent.

Lady Grange was ten months on the island before she tasted real bread. She complained that she lacked shoes and stockings and other necessities, to which Alexander countered that he had no orders to provide her with clothes, or with food other than what he and his wife ate themselves. Bread was a rare commodity in the islands, where oatcakes were the normal fare.

Any communication with the outside world was too dangerous to be permitted. Alexander refused even to tell her the name of the island on which she was imprisoned and it was many months before she knew 'whose ground' she was on. When she discovered the name of the nearest minister, she badgered Alexander to invite the Reverend John McLean of neighbouring Uist to come and pray with her 'for the distress' of her family. McLean responded diplomatically that he was bound to pray for everybody in distress, declining the invitation to visit. At least that was what was relayed back to Lady Grange. 'He had but ane eight mile ferry to cross,' she wrote in her 1741 letter, 'but whether Alex told him I was there I am not positive.'

In the same letter she claims that she attempted to escape from Heskeir by boat, but the man she had bribed ran off with her money. The Sobieski Stuarts weigh in with accusations that she behaved as badly on Heskeir as she had done in Edinburgh, and that on one occasion she had aimed a loaded pistol at her host and on another had thrown a lighted candle at her hostess and attempted to stab her with a knife.

What is certain is that after a year of her company, Alexander Macdonald, the loyal clansman, had had enough. He went off to see Sir Alexander to tell him that he considered it a sin to keep Lady Grange as a prisoner. He returned with real bread and the information that Sir Alexander also repented of meddling in the affair but did not know how to get out of it. In May 1734 Sir Alexander, in Uist on estate business, had better news for the tacksman. Lady Grange would soon be taken away from him. On 14 June 1734 two brothers, John and Norman MacLeod, from Northtown, *Baile mu Thuath*, on the island of Pabbay in the Sound of Harris, arrived at Heskeir in their galley, bearing a letter ordering Alexander to 'give up the cargo that was in his hands'. Alexander showed it to Lady Grange and told her he did not know where she was being taken, which may well have been the case.

The fewer people who could provide information on her whereabouts the better. John MacLeod told her it was the Orkney Islands, which was a lie. But Alexander Macdonald must surely have had his suspicions. The MacLeods were not only tacksmen on Pabbay to the MacLeod chief, they managed the stewardship of distant St Kilda on his behalf. Perhaps he preferred not to be the bearer of bad tidings. Lady Grange would find out soon enough.

'I was in great miserie in the Husker,' Lady Grange was to write later, 'but I'm ten times worse and worse here.' Lady Grange's new home was indeed St Kilda.

CHAPTER 15
The Male Confederacy

They said ten times worse of me when that damn'd Woman went from
Edinburgh than they can say now; for they said it was all my contrivance,
and that it was my servants that took her away; but I defy'd them then, as
I do now, and do declare to you, upon honour, that I do not know what is
become of that Woman, where she is, or who takes care of her; but if I had
contrived, and assisted, and saved my Lord Grange from that devil who
threatened every day to murder him and his children, I would not think
shame of it before God, or man, and where she is, I wish and hope that she
may never be seen again, to torment my worthy Friend.
Letter to 'Cusine Thom', Beaufort, 16 September 1732, Lord Lovat

DISTURBING GOSSIP ABOUT his cousin, Lord Lovat, has reached the ears
of Thomas Fraser, a lawyer in Edinburgh. Disturbing enough for him to
write to his kinsman, perhaps to warn him of the nature of the stories,
perhaps to discover if there is any truth in them. There are two stories in
particular which are 'the talk of the causey' in the capital; one regarding
a woman who has sworn a child against Lord Lovat before the Kirk
Treasurer; the other concerns the disappearance of Lady Grange.

Writing in reply from his castle at Beaufort in September 1732, Lovat
fairly bristles. He assures 'Cusine Thom' that there is no substance to
either allegation. His letter has obviously been written in a furious rage.
Even his copperplate deserts him as he sets his cousin right on the facts,
and directs his venom against his accusers. The woman who had the
temerity to name him as the father of her child is 'a strumpet who
would have difficulty in naming any one man as the father of her child'.
As for Mr Hope of Rankeillour, the 'insolent fellow' who had enquired
what exactly had happened to Lady Grange:

I would advise him not to meddle with me, for the moment that I can prove that he attacts my character and reputation by any calumnie I'll certainly pursue him for *Scandalum Magnatum*. The punishment of which is if proven perpetuall imprisonment, and forfaulture of estate and moveables, which will render him as miserable as he deserves by acting such a villainus part as he does, upon the whole I am very easie upon that subject, for my enemies can't hurt me if they would, and I think it my honour to be attact'd upon Lord Grange's account, and if he was at Edinburgh he would answer for himself, and so I am sure will every man that is attact'd upon his account and I hope come off with triumph.

Thomas Hope of Rankeillour, as lawyer and kinsman, felt a double duty of concern to ensure that Lady Grange was being treated with due care and consideration. One of her last acts, a day or two before she expected to leave Edinburgh for London, had been to call at his house and leave in his care a 'factory', making him in effect her lawyer; a factory being defined, according to *The Concise Scots Dictionary*, as 'authority granted to a person to act on behalf of another, a deed conferring this'. Even armed with this authority, however, it would be advisable for Hope to watch how he challenged Lord Grange or his powerful friends.

Although Hope had been party to the original discussions for the separation of the Granges he had been kept in ignorance of the real circumstances of Lady Grange's imprisonment. However as an astute man with no illusions about the people with whom he had lately been dealing, he would be unlikely to believe that Simon Fraser, Lord Lovat, had no hand in her removal. Cousin Thom too might take some convincing, since Lovat's involvement was known to enough people to ensure that the information would inevitably be passed on. His guilt has since been acknowledged by a succession of commentators.

Carlyle puts the blame jointly on Lord Lovat and the Laird of MacLeod, 'the first as being the most famous plotter in the kingdom, and the second as equally unprincipled'. Maidment too has no doubt of Lovat's participation. The Sobieski Stuarts are certain that he was in charge of the principal movements of Lady Grange's abduction. By the time they arrived in Scotland in the 1820s, the story was history, but their closeness to the families involved, the Frasers in particular, and

Loch Hourn, where a sloop took Lady Grange off the Scottish mainland and out to the Monach Islands. Aquatint (1815) by William Daniell.

their Jacobite sympathies, give their evidence particular weight. Taking the view that Lady Grange was unworthy of sympathy, they list 'the confederates who have come to our knowledge', all long dead, obviating any possibility of legal redress. Their list is headed by the Macdonald and MacLeod clan chiefs, Alexander Macdonald of Sleat and Norman MacLeod of Dunvegan, together with Simon Fraser, Lord Lovat. There follow the names of John Macdonell of Glengarry, John MacLeod of Muiravonside, advocate, Roderick MacLeod of Berneray, Writer to the Signet, and Aeneas Macdonell of Scothouse. Macdonell's residence on the shores of Loch Nevis had been the initial choice for Lady Grange's embarkation from the Scottish mainland before the switch was made to Loch Hourn. All of the men on the Sobieskis' list were in some way related. As well as being Lord Lovat's nephew Norman MacLeod was the brother-in-law of Alexander Macdonald. Aeneas Macdonell was the uncle of John Macdonell, and his wife was Roderick MacLeod's aunt, while John and Roderick MacLeod were cousins. Alexander Macdonald was in addition the son-in-law of Lord Dun. With such a

89

close-knit web of family connections stretching across Scotland from Edinburgh to the Western Isles, what hope of escape was there for Lady Grange?

When David Laing, the noted antiquarian, presented Lady Grange's 1738 letter from St Kilda before a meeting of the Society of Antiquaries of Scotland on 4 June 1874, he too fingered Lovat as the prime mover in the kidnapping and removal of Lady Grange. Even though he had in his possession Lovat's 1732 letter denying any involvement, 'Any assertions or denials on the part of a man who was devoid of all principle can carry little weight,' Laing told the meeting. 'It required the influence and bold resources of such a man as Lovat, rather than her husband, to have attempted and carried out such a scheme.'

But the most telling evidence against Lovat comes from Lady Grange herself. She feared and resented the man she mockingly called her husband's master. In her letters from St Kilda she mentions several clan names, but it is the Fraser connection which runs through her testimony like a prominent line of colour in a clan tartan. If she is to be believed, Lovat servants played a particularly cold-blooded and cruel part in her abduction; she writes that while she was a prisoner at Pomais Lord Lovat came frequently through Stirling and met with Foster and James Fraser 'to concert matters about me'. On 12 August Lord Lovat's page, Peter Fraser arrived, a signal for her forcible removal three days later.

While the Sobieski Stuarts place Lovat in overall command, they identify three men as sharing the responsibility of transferring Lady Grange from Edinburgh to Heskeir: Roderick MacLeod, given probably the most dangerous section from Edinburgh to Clan Donald land; John Macdonell of Glengarry from the handover point north of Loch Ness to the coast; and Sir Alexander Macdonald of Sleat, from the coast to Heskeir. The leaders of this well-planned operation apparently never considered what might have seemed an easier option. Why was Lady Grange not simply killed? But Lord Grange would never have countenanced such a solution. A devout Christian, he was troubled enough to have broken one Commandment, without breaking another. Lady Grange was still his wife until she died a natural death, although after the separation he never again referred to her as such. She became to him 'that creature'.

CHAPTER 16

St Kilda and Martin Martin

*After dinner to-day, we talked of the extraordinary fact of Lady Grange's
being sent to St Kilda, and confined there for several years, without any
means of relief. Dr Johnson said, if McLeod could let it be known that he had
such a place for naughty ladies, he might make it a very profitable island.*
Journal of a Tour to the Hebrides, James Boswell

EASY ENOUGH FOR Dr Johnson, sitting in the comfort of Dunvegan
Castle in Skye after a good dinner on Sunday 19 September 1773, to
make a cheap joke at the expense of Lady Grange. Did he give a thought
for the real woman and the conditions she had to endure on St Kilda?
How would he have fared, uprooted from his cushioned urban lifestyle
to be isolated, against his will, in the harsh environment of a remote
Hebridean island? How would he have coped with having access to
very few books, conversation limited to the one English-speaker, no
delicacies once taken for granted and plain fare supplied at the whim
of MacLeod's steward on his annual visit?

Was he aware that Lady Grange had been clandestinely buried on
the very island where he was now being regally entertained, or that
she had lived there as a prisoner of the MacLeods, who had paid out
£30 annually to a local cottar to provide her with board and lodgings,
far removed in quality and comfort from those he was currently
enjoying?

Johnson could probably plead ignorance of Lady Grange's tragic
last years on Skye: that particular part of her life is unlikely to have
cropped up in the conversation round the table at Dunvegan. Boswell
was hardly better informed. In a footnote to his reference to Lady
Grange in his *Journal of a Tour to the Hebrides* he erroneously records

Dunvegan Castle, Skye, seat of the chiefs of the Clan MacLeod.
Aquatint (1815) by William Daniell.

that after Lady Grange was removed from St Kilda, 'she was conveyed to MacLeod's island of Herries, where she died'. Both Johnson and Boswell, however, were well acquainted with Martin Martin's *A Description of the Western Isles of Scotland* (1703), which sets out a detailed account of life in these then remote islands. Johnson had read it while still very young. Indeed its influence is said to have sparked off his lifelong interest in Scotland. Boswell even had the book with him in his luggage, having borrowed the Advocates Library copy before leaving Edinburgh for their Highland tour.

Martin's books about the Western Isles were early attempts to provide information on the natural history and culture of the islands off the west coast of Scotland to a general reading public which was abysmally ignorant of such matters. Born and reared in Skye with Gaelic as his first language, Martin had graduated Master of Arts from Edinburgh University in 1681. While living in the Scottish capital he had experienced at first hand the ignorance of the Lowland Scot regarding the Highlands and Islands. 'Many that live in the South of Scotland know no more of the Western Isles than the Natives of Italy,' he complained. He set out to remedy the situation with his fact-finding voyages and the books which resulted from them, encouraged in his enterprise by Sir Robert Sibbald, the Geographer Royal of Scotland, John Adair, the mapmaker, and James Sutherland, Keeper of the Botanic Garden, together with influential members of the Royal Society in London.

Yet even Martin, the Gaelic insider, would not have contemplated extending his time on St Kilda beyond a three-week summer visit. The Celtic west was no longer somewhere he cared to live. He had grown to enjoy the stimulus of 'civilised' society in Edinburgh and London too much. How could anyone think that exile in such a place as St Kilda would be bearable to a woman from Lady Grange's background, or that confining her there could ever be justified? No matter how 'naughty' she had been.

Martin's visit predates Lady Grange's arrival by only 37 years. Though there would be changes and one major catastrophe in the intervening period, his detailed description of the island and its inhabitants is still an essential read for anyone wishing to understand the difficulties and challenges which awaited Lady Grange on St Kilda. Even today a successful landing from the sea cannot be guaranteed. After several unsuccessful attempts Martin finally landed there in the company of John Campbell, minister in Harris, who had been asked by the MacLeod chief to attend to the spiritual needs of the inhabitants. The two men set sail on the afternoon of 29 May 1697, with the weather set fair and a gentle breeze blowing. Scarcely had they left the harbour, however, than the minister, observing the whiteness of the waves, was expressing fears of a coming storm. Although the crew was dismissive, the minister proved only too prescient. It took three days and, according to Martin, a liberal application of aqua vitae to the oarsmen, before the island was finally reached. The only possible landing-place along the inhospitable shoreline of towering cliffs was at Village Bay, near the islanders' houses. But even then it was only on the north side of the bay that the rocks were low enough to enable visitors to come ashore. When the tides and winds were favourable or when there was a perfect calm (which, then as now, was rare) a boat could be hauled ashore over the rocks. This involved all the able-bodied islanders of both sexes, under the command of a crier, pulling on a rope attached to the prow.

Martin's boat was observed first by a few of the St Kildans who were trapping sea-birds on the clifftops. They proceeded to out-run the boat to break the news of the imminent arrival of visitors. 'I was obliged to turn away mine eyes,' Martin writes, 'lest I should have the unpleasant spectacle of some of them tumbling down into the sea.' By the time he reached the bay a 'parcel of the inhabitants' had assembled on the Saddle, the name given to the low, seaweed-covered rocks. His boat was held off the rocks by long poles, while two of the welcoming party waded into the sea to carry him and the minister ashore on their shoulders.

Lady Grange makes no mention of the manner in which she arrived on St Kilda. Perhaps she was fortunate enough to be pulled ashore, dry-shod, in the MacLeod brothers' galley; if the weather dictated otherwise, she would have found herself once more carried to a place to which she had no desire to go.

The inaccessibility of the island impinged on every aspect of life there. Visitors were a rare occurence, and the few islanders who left their home returned with tales of wonderment. To them, according to Martin, a looking-glass was a prodigy, wall hangings were condemned as vain and superfluous, and the Lowland dress of MacLeod's wife was too strange even to be described. What would the islanders make of Lady Grange, and she of them? It hardly seems likely there would be a meeting of tastes, let alone a meeting of minds.

CHAPTER 17

Roderick the Impostor

One of the most interesting individuals in the history of Hirt.
St Kilda: Church, Visitors, and 'Natives', Michael Robson

THE INACCESSIBILITY OF St Kilda presented a particular difficulty for the Church of Scotland but the moral wellbeing of the islanders, and particularly the children, concerned the local synod and periodically they drew the matter to the attention of the General Assembly in Edinburgh. The Reformation had never taken hold as firmly in the islands of the western seaboard of Scotland as on the mainland. The Synod of Argyll and the Isles had been established in 1638 with theoretical control of an area stretching from Rona and Lewis in the north to Kintyre in the south (with even some coastal areas of Inverness-shire thrown in for good measure), but it lacked the resources and the manpower to spiritually police such a vast territory.

There were corners where popery and paganism, twin evils in the eyes of the Kirk, continued to have a claim on the loyalties of the local population. St Kilda was one such corner. Neither priest nor minister lived there and marriages, baptisms and burials had to be conducted by the islanders themselves. All of these ceremonies included customs which were unlikely to meet with the approval of the Synod of Argyll and the Isles.

Marriage vows were sworn on the island's brass crucifix in the presence of the officer, the local representative of MacLeod's steward. Baptisms, with the participation of a sponsor (*goistidh*) and a godmother (*banaghoistidh*) were conducted on a Saturday in the superstitious belief that thereby the children would live. Burials were accompanied by excessive wailing, dangerously reminiscent of the practice known as the corronach, which the Synod of Argyll condemned as 'unseemly for use by any true Christian Kirk where the comfortable Resurrection of the dead was preached and professed'. Such a practice was, in the synod's view, the province only of ignorant women.

The arrival of the Reverend John Campbell on St Kilda in June 1697 was an opportunity for couples to have their marriage conducted in a manner more acceptable to the church – hence the minister's particularly busy day on 17 June, when no less than 15 couples were united in holy matrimony, pledging their troth on the island's crucifix. According to Martin it was a joyous occasion, with all the couples taking part in a country dance after the ceremony, to the music of a bagpipe.

It was perhaps not the right time to suggest dispensing with the crucifix used for swearing decisive oaths and making marriage vows but its presence must have troubled the Protestant minister. Martin takes the view that the islanders, while holding it in great reverence, did not worship it. However, its days were numbered: in 1727, in the little book *A Description of St Kilda*, the use of the crucifix is listed as one of several 'superstitious practices' which had been done away with.

Martin and Campbell had further business to undertake on behalf of the Kirk authorities. News had reached Edinburgh that a false prophet had acquired a regrettable influence over the islanders. This was Ruairidh Mhòr, a red-haired, handsome St Kildan who surpassed all the other inhabitants of the island in his strength and climbing ability. He was, moreover, a bard with the gift of the second-sight who claimed to receive teachings direct from St John the Baptist. His teachings included praying to personal saints, observing a strict Friday fast and doing penances; pregnant women were encouraged to pray to the Virgin Mary for a safe delivery. These practices chimed in comfortably with the old Catholic faith and Ruairidh Mhòr might have continued undisturbed had it not been for Martin and Campbell. The need to counteract his influence was as crucial a reason for their visit as Campbell's pastoral mission or Martin's desire to gather information for his book. Both men subjected Ruairidh to a rigorous examination of his beliefs. The illiterate islander was no match for them. Compelled to make a public recantation, he was further humiliated by being forced to take part in

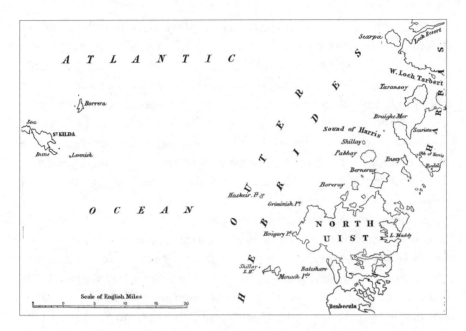

Map showing St Kilda in relation to Heskeir and North Uist.

the physical scattering of the stones of the wall he had built round the
holy ground he had named John the Baptist's Bush. The islanders were
persuaded to acknowledge the error of their ways and what remained
of Ruairidh's reputation was fatally damaged – or so his two inquisitors
hoped – when the story was circulated that he had debauched women
in private while teaching them the Virgin Mary's hymn.

Martin never refers to Ruairidh Mhòr by his name but always by
the belittling title of 'Roderick the Impostor'. Michael Robson, in his
magisterial work on St Kilda, is of the opinion that Martin's account
is coloured with the language of religious hostility and verges on the
hypocritical, since he dismisses Ruairidh's curious religious forms as
ridiculous, yet presents without condemnation other superstitious
practices which might seem far more so. Martin was himself torn
between two worlds: the darker Celtic world to which Ruairidh
belonged with his second-sight and capacity to see visions, and the
modern scientific world. Martin could not help feeling himself superior
to the St Kildans with their limited knowledge of so many things, from
reading and writing to medicine and fire-making. Yet he liked to think

of them as in some ways superior, a Hebridean version of the primitive but noble savage. His decision to favour St Kilda over Hirte as the name of the island is symptomatic of this personal dilemma. Hirt, or Hirte, from an Old Norse word *hirtir*, meaning stags, was the name used by the inhabitants themselves and by the neighbouring Gaelic-speaking communities. St Kilda is also thought to have Old Norse roots, either from *skildir* meaning shields, or *kilde,* a spring or well, of which there were several on the island. The name was misread, however, when it appeared in an early map, leading to the creation of a non-existent saint.

St Kilda was taken up by continental cartographers for sea-maps, and it is this fabricated name which Martin chose to use for the title of his book. Possibly he did so because he considered it might appeal more to the educated reading public for whom he was writing. He was after all intending to dedicate his book on the island to Charles Montague, Chancellor of His Majesty's Exchequer and President of the Royal Society in London. Whatever the motivation, Martin's choice was decisive. Hirt, Hirta or Hirte would linger on, used mainly by Gaelic-speaking locals for the inhabited main island. But to the world at large the name was St Kilda, and that is the name that Lady Grange writes at the top of her 1738 letter.

When Martin and Campbell finally left they took Ruairidh with them, handing him into the custody of the steward in Pabbay to await trial for his beliefs. Martin claims that the islanders had attempted to prevent Ruairidh's departure for fear his presence on board the boat would bring about a storm and endanger the lives of the other passengers. It might have been that they did not want him to leave, a possibility Martin prefers not to consider. Even without his physical presence Ruairidh Mhòr's teachings survived on St Kilda and 'manie of his prosolits' were still living in 1705, according to a letter of that date. By then the Kirk, convinced that the presence of a minister, or at least a catechist, was essential to secure the island in the Protestant fold, had appointed Alexander Buchan to the task. His desperate letters to his employers provide a chilling account of the conditions on St Kilda.

CHAPTER 18
St Kilda and Alexander Buchan

The island of Hirta has been much upon my heart and I have denyed
my Self the Ease and other Worldly accommodations I might have had
elsewhere to serve the Intrest of the Gospell in that Place, and I bless the
Lord not without some success.
Letter to the SSPCK, 1710, Alexander Buchan

OPINIONS MAY DIFFER on the merits of Alexander Buchan, the man
who volunteered to take on the position of constant catechist on St
Kilda in 1704. Robson considers him to be 'as heroic a religious figure
as any of a different kind that had gone before him', while John Lorne
Campbell characterises him as 'a bigoted, narrow, ignorant, difficult
person, married to a complaining wife'. But there is no denying Buchan's
Christian commitment. Even so it is impossible not to wonder whether
he, and perhaps more importantly his wife, had any real idea of what
they would face. Although the Buchans possessed some experience
of life on islands on the west coast of Scotland, nothing could have
prepared them for St Kilda.

Buchan was born in the Caithness parish of Halkirk and worked
there for several years as a catechist, before moving to Argyll to take up
the post of schoolmaster at Ederline in Kilmichael Glassary. It is more
than likely that his wife Katherine was the daughter of Daniel Campbell,
minister there. After a year of schoolmastering he returned to what was
obviously his real love – expounding and examining on the essentials
of the Protestant faith. He served as a catechist for two years on Jura,
followed by a year on Mull, before returning to Caithness to continue
his work in Thurso. There he and Katherine might have settled if news
had not reached him of the perilous state of the Protestant faith on St
Kilda. Buchan made the momentous decision to travel to Edinburgh

and volunteer his services. Both as a fluent Gaelic-speaker and a convinced Presbyterian, he would have been a strong candidate for the St Kilda post, even if there had been any other applicants. There were none. However he lacked the university education which might have persuaded the Kirk authorities to offer him ordination to the ministry before his departure. Their failure to do so would critically undermine his authority in the eyes of the islanders, who continued the practice of conducting baptisms, marriages, and burials for themselves.

The Assembly Commission had supplied him with an initial payment of 200 merks, together with a selection of what they considered to be suitable books and a letter to be delivered to the Synod of Argyll requesting that a letter be written to MacLeod, proprietor of St Kilda, enlisting his support for the catechist and suggesting the laird provide a viaticum of 100 pounds Scots (approximately £8 sterling) to speed Buchan on his way there 'with all diligence before the Season is over'.

Nothing could more perfectly illustrate the Commission's profound ignorance of communication problems in the Outer Hebrides, let alone the limited transport opportunities available to travellers to St Kilda. It was already late in the summer when the Buchans, with their two young children, set out for St Kilda and it was early November when they arrived on the island of Pabbay in the Sound of Harris, after a tedious and troublesome journey. It was now far too late in the year to attempt a crossing to St Kilda and the family were obliged to over-winter on Pabbay at their own expense. It was not an auspicious start.

Buchan was already becoming aware of the difficulties he would face on St Kilda. 'Some ministers told me they would not venter to go ther for a thousand pounds and tarrie on[e] year,' he writes in the first of two doom-laden letters from Pabbay to the Moderator of the General Assembly. The overriding problem of a lack of money is a recurring theme in his communications to the 'godly wisdoms' in Edinburgh. Wise they might have been, but they lacked any comprehension of living conditions on St Kilda, or of the poverty of the population. They had no appreciation of Buchan's limited facility to travel (he was even censured for failing to attend presbytery meetings) or of the effect which a once-a-year postal service, courtesy of MacLeod's steward, had on their catechist's ability to keep them as informed as they demanded to

Sketched by Sir Thomas Acland in 1812, the old village of St Kilda predates the removal of the islanders to the 'street' of houses.

be on the success, or otherwise, of his work. Only a saint or a hermit would not have complained. Being neither, but being instead a feisty lady, Katherine Buchan was driven to make several visits to Edinburgh over the years to fight her husband's corner and to seek to improve the lot of her growing family. Each visit meant leaving the island with the steward's boat in the late summer and returning the following year. Buchan himself made only one visit to Edinburgh during almost 25 years' service on St Kilda, travelling off the island in 1709 with the steward's boat, and taking with him Finlay MacDonald and Murdo Campbell, the two pupils he had taught to read. Perhaps he hoped to impress his employers with their progress, and certainly when he returned to the island the following summer it was as a fully-fledged minister, having been ordained in St Giles by the Presbytery of Edinburgh on 15 March 1710. His ministerial remit, however, was carefully confined to St Kilda 'and other Remote places'.

That same month the Scottish Society for the Propagation of Christian Knowledge, which had been set up the previous year, agreed to employ Buchan as schoolmaster in St Kilda and his annual salary was increased to 300 merks. This might have heralded some improvement in the family's financial problems, if a reliable system of payment had been available. Unfortunately this was not the case. In 1713 Buchan had received none of his salary for the previous three years (900 merks) and owed 760 merks 'on tick' for the overpriced goods supplied by the steward.

According to *A Description of St Kilda,* the main reason for the islanders' poverty was in fact the steward's annual visit. Compulsory maintenance of his party for most of the summer had become an unsustainable burden on the islanders and the rent in kind which he carried away was 'almost all they should live upon through the year'. Later editions of the book carry the name of Alexander Buchan as the author and certainly Buchan took with him to Edinburgh in 1709 a little book which was all his own work. This first attempt at publication failed and the work was substantially altered by the time it was published in 1727, with much of the text supplied by another, anonymous hand. The comments on the steward's levies are, however, believed to be Buchan's and there is no doubt that the minister grew to sympathise with the lot of his parishioners, whose poverty he shared. In his opinion far too many unnecessary deaths were occurring on Hirta because of malnutrition.

A greater disaster, however, was about to befall St Kilda. In the summer of 1727 a native of the island died of a high fever during a summer visit to Harris. Donald MacDonald's body was taken back to the island for burial together with his few belonging. There is a story that his disconsolate sister embraced his clothes. His death had profound and unexpected consequences: St Kilda's only recorded outbreak of smallpox raged through the mean and unhygienic houses.

Out of a population of 122, only 42 survived through to the following spring, 77 having died of smallpox and three of other causes. Among the survivors were three men and eight boys who owed their lives to being trapped on Stac an Armin. They had gone there before the smallpox outbreak in order to harvest solan geese (gannets) and should have been collected a fortnight later but no boat came: there were already insufficient able-bodied men left to effect a rescue and they were forced to overwinter on the inhospitable stac.

St Kilda's dreadful plight was not discovered until the steward's boat arrived in the spring of 1728. The Reverend Daniel Macaulay, minister of Bracadale in Skye, who arrived shortly afterwards for a much postponed inspection of Buchan's work, was also greeted with the devastating news. He reported back to Edinburgh on both the smallpox and on the island's minister.

Despite the ordeal so recently suffered by the islanders, the work of the Lord still required to be done. Surviving heads of families had to be quizzed by the visiting minister regarding the frequency of the Sacrament of the Lord's Supper, the diligence of Buchan's catechising, his success in teaching reading, his commitment to visiting his flock. Had they any complaints against Mr Buchan? They answered that they had none.

In his final report, the Reverend Daniel Macaulay damned Buchan with faint praise, judging that he was well enough read in the Scriptures but otherwise poorly qualified, and that his 'stock of prudence' was not large. Having examined all the books in Buchan's custody, he found most of them to be useless, noting that they were scattered in moist places through his house – though he did have the grace to add that the family 'lacked a press' in which to keep them.

Kinder comments came from a fellow minister, the Reverend James Campbell of Kilbrandon, who had received a letter from Buchan detailing the desolateness of his parish and the extreme poverty of his private circumstances. Campbell was moved enough to write twice to the SSPCK in Edinburgh early in 1729, pleading for charity in the case of 'poor old Mr Buchan', who had spent his life in 'that desolate Corner'.

It was already too late. Alexander Buchan had died on St Kilda in February 1729, possibly a late victim of the smallpox outbreak, or perhaps from frailty after 25 years of physical hardship. His death was the final blow for a traumatised community.

Katherine Buchan – she who had taught the women of St Kilda to knit on wires and had introduced the wonders of a cock and hens – left for Edinburgh, to 'Shift for a Livelyhood', as she told the SSPCK in a petition for financial support. Describing herself as destitute, she continued to battle for herself and her six fatherless children for several years, to no great avail.

On St Kilda recovery was slow. Some incomers were persuaded to settle there from Skye, Harris, and North Uist but even by 1758 there were fewer than a hundred willing to attempt the task of making a living there. This then was the island, depleted in population and still in shock from recent events, to which Lady Grange came in the summer of 1734. She herself was under no illusions as to the quality of life in her new home. 'It is a viled neasty stinking poor Isle,' she wrote. 'No body lives in it but the poor natives.'

CHAPTER 19

The Lady on the Island

She drank as heavily as her meagre supplies of whisky allowed and every
night would wander down by the dark shore like a wild swan with a
damaged wing, bemoaning her captivity. Gradually madness returned and,
rising up as the pitiless Atlantic wind, blew until the dispersal of her senses
was complete.
Island on the Edge of the World, Charles Maclean

Lady Grange is said to have devoted her whole time on St Kilda to weeping
and wrapping up letters round pieces of cork bound with yarn, to try if
any favourable wind would waft them to some Christian, to inform some
humane person where she resided, in expectation of carrying tidings to her
friends in Edinburgh.
The Life and Death of St Kilda, Tom Steel

WAS LADY GRANGE driven mad by the conditions of her imprisonment?
Did she truly spend her time in tears, casting letters into the sea in an
early, futile version of the St Kilda mail-boat? Contemporary sources
have their own agendas for painting the picture as bright, or as dark,
as possible, and Lady Grange's own account certainly falls into the
dark category. According to her second St Kilda letter, she survived in
a very miserable condition. No provision was made for her except for
two pecks of flour and what the island could afford – a supply of milk
and a little barley. She would have died 'from want of meat' if the new
minister and his wife, who arrived on the island shortly after her, had
not taken care of her.

She makes no comment on the kind of house provided, but complains
that she had no one to wait on her who understood her. Again the
minister and his wife came to her aid, explaining Lady Grange's

wishes to the little Highland girl who served her. A manservant who understood a little English completed the household. She described him as being not only ill-natured but half-witted as well. One day he even drew out his 'durk' to kill her – an incident which might indicate that Lady Grange's old knack of upsetting the servants had survived the journey from Preston to St Kilda unimpaired.

A much more comforting account of her circumstances emerges from statements taken on St Kilda around October 1740 by Donald MacLeod of Berneray. Donald was not only baron-bailie of Harris for the MacLeod chief but he was also the younger brother of John MacLeod of Muiravonside, who had been so involved in the removal of Lady Grange from Edinburgh. By then Roderick MacLennan, the minister who had been so helpful to Lady Grange, had left the island, and it was to counteract any concern he might raise on her behalf that MacLeod was dispatched to St Kilda. The information he was given was that Lady Grange had been treated well: the milk she drank was from the best cows, and according to the testimony of her servant, Florence MacLeod, was so abundant that she was able to make fresh butter and still have milk left over to give to needy families.

Lady Grange's house was 40 feet long with an inner room and a chimney, and the luxury of two windows. Her furniture included a curtained bed, an armchair and a table. She was provided with a plentiful supply of clothes and an ample store of provisions, including spirits. MacLeod's informants felt it was necessary to add that the lady was addicted to liquor, as well as to outbursts of uncontrolled bad temper. Was this just the obligatory smear, another stone to be added to the cairn dedicated to the destruction of Lady Grange's character? It was unlikely, after all, that the islanders would not be aware of the kind of answers expected of them.

In the business of smearing none are more zealous than the Sobieski Stuarts, who blacken her name with allegations of drunken behaviour and claim that only three days after her arrival on the island she was found lying beside the rum cask in a condition which obliged the steward and his servants to lift her from the ground and carry her to bed; not only did her intemperance scandalise the islanders, she beat her servants with whatever came to hand and on one occasion attempted to

'Cleit 85', which marks the probable site of Lady Grange's house on St Kilda.

take a loaded pistol hanging above the steward's bed while he slept.

With access to MacLeod sources and most probably to the 1740 statements, the Sobieski Stuarts confidently itemise Lady Grange's annual provision from the island itself, claiming that they had taken the details from instructions set down in a book by MacLeod's steward. According to these instructions, she was to be given 12 stone of butter and cheese, a cow, 12 sheep, 8 bolls of meal (a boll being a measure weighing 140 lb), 12 lambs, one and a half bolls of malt, one boll of barley for broth, hens' eggs and fish *ad libitum*, 2 Scots pints of milk daily, 6 stones of candles, and peats *ad libitum*.

A curious omission from this list are the sea-birds and their eggs which were so central to the islanders' own diet. In the past these had been generously bestowed on visitors. Martin's men were each given a daily allowance of at least 40 assorted eggs as well as other provisions, and Martin himself calculated that 16,000 eggs in all had been provided for those of his boat and the steward's *birlinn* – some 60 men – during their three-week stay.

Birds and eggs were customarily preserved under a covering of turf or peat ash in 'cleits', stone outhouses where they might be left for as long as eight months. They were nothing if not an acquired taste and several of Martin's men fell ill after eating eggs. Lady Grange perhaps had cause to be grateful to Katherine Buchan for her introduction of a cock and hens to the island. For the first four years of her imprisonment she was also supplied with the following imported goods: 1 lb of tea, 1 stone of sugar, 6 pecks of wheat, and one anker (in Scots measure, 4 gallons) of spirits. Thereafter her allowance of imported goods was augmented to 2 lb of tea, 6 lb each of prunes and raisins, 3 lb of rice, 2 ankers of brandy, 4 wheaten loaves, and 12 bottles of white wine. Such liberality from the hand of the steward would have amazed Alexander Buchan.

The Sobieski Stuarts also provide details of Lady Grange's clothes: gowns, cloaks, velvet hoods, shoes and stockings, twilled petticoats, a large number of waistcoats and handkerchiefs, muslin and cambric head-dresses and a camlet cloak. There are even detailed descriptions of her furniture: a table, a chair with cushion, standing bed with curtains, a new wool bed, a feather bed, four pairs of fine blankets, five pairs of sheets, candlesticks, pots, pans and dishes. Apart from the conundrum of wondering how such a large amount of impedimenta could have been conveyed to the island with the steward's *birlinn* – let alone how it could be accommodated in a St Kildan house – the sheer volume of supplies must also be questioned, especially those provided from the island itself. This was a different, less prosperous, island than the one which heaped such hospitality on Martin and his crew, with fewer adults to harvest the birds, cultivate the land, and look after the livestock. It seems likely that the Sobieski Stuarts' lists were drawn up for the consumption and reassurance of posterity, rather than for the consumption and comfort of Lady Grange.

CHAPTER 20
Living with the Natives

The house is seven paces long, of my paces, and three and a half wide, which is about 20 feet by 10. Like the rest of the houses, it is divided in the centre by a partition of rude loose stone. In one of these apartments sat Finlay McDonald every night for seven years, and Lady Grange in the other... the entire of her ladyship's accommodation being ten feet semilunar!
Sketches of the Island of St Kilda, Lachlan MacLean

ON 25 JULY 1838 the steamship *Vulcan* arrived on an excursion to St Kilda. Among the passengers was Lachlan MacLean, who took the opportunity to visit the ruins of the hut where 'the celebrated Lady Grange spent seven years of her tragical existence'. His guide was the grandson of Finlay MacDonald who had attended Lady Grange. The conversation, as recorded by MacLean, provides an alternative, more believable, account of the reality of Lady Grange's life on St Kilda.

Finlay MacDonald, the son of the island's officer, was one of the two boys who had been taught to read by Buchan. He had accompanied Buchan to Edinburgh in 1709 and attended his ordination in St Giles in March 1710 before they both returned to St Kilda. He is also presumably the manservant characterised by Lady Grange as half-witted and ill-natured. But over the years they seem to have learned to co-exist. According to his grandson Lady Grange found pleasure in listening to Finlay's native tales and romances, having acquired Gaelic 'tolerably well'. When she was taken from the island she carried with her the seat of twisted straw, a luxury object in St Kilda, which Finlay had made for her, leaving him the substantial sum of 12 shillings in silver in lieu. Lachlan MacLean was also informed that during her time on St Kilda Lady Grange slept through the day, except when she took a solitary ramble 'to converse with grief and the roaring ocean'. At night she never slept.

Like Buchan, Lady Grange was well aware of the poverty of the islanders and did what little she could to alleviate their suffering. She would never, however, have stepped out of the mistress–servant relationship and it is unlikely she would ever have visited St Kildans in their own homes. Even Buchan, the professional Christian, confessed in one of his early letters that he found it difficult to stay long enough to pray in a St Kildan house because of the smell.

When the *Vulcan* dropped anchor in Village Bay in 1838 the islanders were in the throes of a housing upgrade. This had been brought about jointly by the philanthropy of Sir Thomas Dyke Acland – a Devon man who had visited in 1812 and again in 1834, and had been appalled by the conditions in which the islanders lived – and by the energy of the Reverend Neil MacKenzie, minister on the island from 1830–44, who set about spending the £20 bequeathed by Acland 'to encourage the people to build better houses'.

It was not until the late 1830s that the move was begun from the original village to the present-day iconic street site. The reluctance of the islanders to abandon their cosy, if smelly, old houses hindered 'progress'. While in the past they had slept in beds built into the thick walls of their houses, they would now be given free-standing modern bedsteads. Instead of the more sheltered position of the old village, the new houses would be built in line with each other, end-on to the sea. These houses still punctuate the present 'street' of 1860 dwellings, and were later used as byres, stores and working spaces.

When the passengers from the *Vulcan* came to view the St Kildans and their way of life, it was still to the old huddle of houses that they came, for MacLean notes that the houses were 'in one confused cluster'. He captures the occasion in his journal, describing how the party discovered to their astonishment that the outside walls of the houses were ornamented with solan geese, stuck by their bills into the crevices in the stone walls until their feathers would be dry enough for plucking. On the ground lay mangled goose carcasses, 'emitting effluvia the reverse of ambrosial'. It was a ludicrous sight, MacLean writes, to see his fellow passengers, 'every one with his nose in his hand, as if acting a pantomime'. These were the houses inhabited by the St Kildans a hundred years earlier when Lady Grange arrived. Two sketches of the village survive, one by Acland in 1812 and one by William Train, a professional artist who accompanied the travel writer George Atkinson to the island in 1831. Florence MacLeod, the little Highland girl who served Lady Grange would have lived here, returning home every evening.

How far did Florence have to walk from her mistress's house? The National Trust for Scotland identifies 'Cleit 85' as 'said to be the home of Lady Grange'. Although this cleit is on the seaward side of the 'street', it can only have been a 15-minute walk from the old village. However, rather than being her actual dwelling, 'Cleit 85' merely marks its site. The house was already in ruins when visited by Lachlan MacLean in 1838. The RCAHMS booklet *Buildings of St Kilda* states that the structure was demolished in the early 1870s and the present cleit is unlikely to incorporate more than a mere vestige of the original structure. Only the view links us back to Lady Grange.

Sufficiently distant from the old village to acknowledge her superior status, the house would have been the summer residence of MacLeod's steward. When the pressing need arose in 1734 to find accommodation for Lady Grange, the steward's house would have been the only solution. Although she would have to share it with him in the summer and accept the presence of MacDonald as handyman, companion, and guard, the internal partition would have afforded a modicum of privacy for her. Preston House it clearly was not, but it was preferable to the lot of her fellow islanders, who shared their houses throughout the winter with their animals and their accumulated droppings. There may be some substance to the Sobieski Stuarts' story of Lady Grange seeking to remove a loaded pistol from the head of the steward's bed, if they shared a house.

To this single-storey stone cottage with its thatched roof, Roderick MacLennan would have come, one of Lady Grange's few visitors. He had been appointed minister, catechist, and schoolmaster on St Kilda in 1734, arriving on the island with his wife the same summer as Lady Grange.

It is hardly surprising that a friendship would develop between the religiously-minded Lady Grange and the minister – a friendship not without its dangers. The Reverend John McLean of Uist had cannily avoided being drawn into any involvement with her while she was imprisoned on Heskeir. For MacLennan it was much more difficult to ignore her plight. He may have been the better Christian, but he was certainly also the more unwise. His association with Lady Grange and his attempts to help her would end in disaster for his family, and ultimately prove of little assistance.

CHAPTER 21

Roderick MacLennan

He is a serious and devout man, and very painfull and what time he can
spare from his business he is so good as to come and see me.
Letter from St Kilda, 21 January 1741, Lady Grange

At length she obtained a tool, in the person of one of those illiterate and
wretched catechists. The confidante of Lady Grange was one of this class,
evident from the Narrative which he wrote from her dictation which in the
greatest degree was base and slovenly and in some places almost illegible.
Tales of the Century, the Sobieski Stuarts

WHAT IS TO be made of Roderick MacLennan, a man much admired by
Lady Grange and comprehensively trashed by her enemies? According
to the Fasti of the Church of Scotland he was educated at King's College,
Aberdeen, graduating MA on 2 April 1719 and going on to study Divinity
at the University of Edinburgh. Although his place of birth is unknown,
he was a native Gaelic-speaker and it is not surprising to find that by
1727 he was over in the west of Scotland, living in the Lochaber area,
having qualified as a catechist. He is described as 'a pious young man'
by the minister of Kilmallie in a letter to the Royal Bounty Committee
of the General Assembly in Edinburgh, successfully recommending that
MacLennan be paid as a catechist within the bounds of the Presbytery
of Abertarff.

By the spring of 1731 MacLennan himself was looking to move on.
In a letter to the same committee he writes of his desire to be 'useful
in some corner of the world by saving souls'. He even suggests that he
would be willing to go to St Kilda, provided 'due encouragement' was
given – by which he probably meant financial encouragement, since his

View of Village Bay, St Kilda. Lady Grange's house was between the present-day 'street' and the sea, and to the right of the central line of stones.

letter drops several hints about his 'want of fonds'. The spiritual health of St Kilda, which had been without catechist, teacher, or minister since the death of Alexander Buchan, was once more exercising the collective mind of the Kirk. Following the smallpox outbreak the island had been resettled with incomers who had been persuaded to move there from other Hebridean islands, including the Uists and Skye. The population now stood at around 70 and in the opinion of the Synod of Glenelg was in danger of falling back into 'heathnish darkness'.

The difficulty of finding and funding a minister for St Kilda remained unresolved until welcome and unexpected news was given to the SSPCK in December 1733 by John MacLeod of Muiravonside. His uncle Alexander MacLeod, an Edinburgh advocate and a founder member of the Society, had left it the sum of 6,000 merks to ensure the prompt appointment of a minister to St Kilda. With a guaranteed income from the interest on such a sizeable sum the Society felt able to consider the employment of a minister on St Kilda, with additional duties as catechist and schoolmaster, at an annual salary of 450 merks. It was a substantial encouragement, especially for those with a burning desire to save souls for the Protestant cause and little knowledge of the island in which the owners of the souls lived.

Roderick MacLennan was already the preferred candidate, at least by the Presbytery of Skye, who ordained him in the early summer of 1734 specifically with the ministry of St Kilda in mind. He was soon on his way there with half a year's salary in advance, as yet unaware of the presence of the imprisoned wife of Lord Grange, an important figure in Church circles in Edinburgh, or that any involvement with her would bring him into conflict with powerful figures both in the *Gàidhealtachd* and in the Scottish capital.

As minister of St Kilda MacLennan found himself a member of the Presbytery of Long Island, whose meetings were held at Scarista in Harris. This was nearer than Buchan's presbytery meetings in Skye had been but equally impossible to attend. There were other familiar problems. In a letter to the SSPCK in 1738, MacLennan complains that the laird of MacLeod had refused to assist him with the provision of a house and cow's grass. Matters did not improve. When MacLennan left the island the following summer it was for good. In a letter to the Society from Skye in August 1739, he informed them that, discouraged by the harsh treatment his family had received from the steward, he would not be returning to St Kilda. Enclosing details of the number of catechisable persons on the island (50 out of the population of 70) and a list of the children who occasionally attended school, MacLennan was apparently still anxious to be employed by the Society, so long as it was 'Elsewhere'.

One of the Society's responses to this letter was to notify its contents to John MacLeod of Muiravonside, the man who had been instrumental in the arrangements for his uncle's generous bequest to the Society. He was also the man who had allowed his house to be used to accommodate Lady Grange and her kidnappers that first day after her enforced removal from Edinburgh. It is unlikely that the SSPCK was aware of any connection between MacLeod and the disappearance of Lady Grange from Edinburgh. They simply wished to inform him of the unfortunate turn of events on St Kilda, involving the minister whose appointment had been made possible through his uncle's generosity.

But there was an unintended result of the Society's action: MacLeod had now been alerted to the threat of a disaffected minister who was no longer isolated on St Kilda and whose personal knowledge of Lady Grange's misfortunes might prove dangerous. For the moment MacLennan was still living in the *Gàidhealtachd*, but what if he was to go to Edinburgh? The situation required careful management and swift action.

MacLennan did indeed travel to Edinburgh, though not, so far as can be determined, until the following year, when he delivered an account of his time on St Kilda to the SSPCK, detailing the 'discouragements' he had encountered and proposing 'certain expedients' to attract a successor. His report was considered at a committee meeting on 4 December 1740 and later that month the Society wrote to MacLeod asking for help to be given to the next missionary on St Kilda. MacLeod was also asked to use his influence with the laird, which indicated that at this stage the SSPCK perhaps thought MacLennan had grounds for dissatisfaction.

Meanwhile MacLeod had already been very busy. In August he put forward for the Society's consideration a suitable candidate for the vacant position on St Kilda, a Skye schoolmaster with the reassuring surname of MacLeod. By February 1741 with the agreement of the Society and the co-operation of the Presbytery of Skye, Alexander MacLeod was following the same route to ordination as had been taken by MacLennan. He would depart for St Kilda in the summer.

Even more important to MacLeod and his fellow conspirators was the urgent need to collect evidence to neutralise any adverse information which might become public regarding the treatment of Lady Grange. Donald Macleod was selected for the task. Not only was he the baron-bailie of Harris but, as the brother of John Macleod, would be considered a safe pair of hands. He may have been at work on St Kilda by the autumn of 1740 gathering statements to prove that Lady Grange was well looked after and kept in comfort. In addition he would take note of any stories, the more scandalous the better, which could be used to blacken the characters of both Lady Grange and Roderick MacLennan.

By the time the MacLeod laird replied in March 1741 to the SSPCK's letter, reassuring the Society of his zeal to encourage any who might be sent to St Kilda to preach the Gospel, he felt obliged to inform them of more disturbing news. He was now aware of 'certain malicious and vile practices whereof Mr Roderick MacLennan late Minister there had been guilty which are vouched by Documents in the hands of John MacLeod Advocate'. The Sobieski Stuarts provide more detail: MacLennan was alleged to have kicked a pregnant woman, refused the rites of Christianity to those with whom he had quarrelled, denied prayers to a sick woman, and baptism to a dying child. He was accused of planning and sharing the theft of 24 sheep, hiring boys to steal his neighbours' peats and inciting the people against the MacLeod steward. What a sea-change, if it is to be believed, had occurred in the pious young man of the Kilmallie minister's acquaintance. Even his wife does not escape denigration, being 'a bold and impudent scold'. Both husband and wife were also unconnected to the Clan MacLeod, obviously a serious omission on their part.

MacLennan's predicament calls into question the position of the church in the Lady Grange affair. She herself tells us in her 1741 letter that fellow ministers had become angry with MacLennan because of the care and concern he had taken of her. The presbytery in Harris must have known of her presence on their territory, and the Kirk's network of presbyteries and synods could have conveyed news of her imprisonment to Edinburgh, which it appears they never did. Were Kirk leaders reluctant to cross Lord Grange? Or did they believe that his wife really was a madwoman, imprisoned for her own good? MacLennan's sympathy with her plight was certainly not shared by the Kirk or by the SSPCK. Meanwhile the confederacy had collected sufficient 'evidence' – or so they hoped – to invalidate any information the minister might try to communicate.

There still remains the enigma of Lady Grange's two letters, which reached Edinburgh in the winter of 1740. At her request, fair copies were made of the second, much longer letter, and distributed throughout the capital, becoming 'the talk of coffee houses and tea tables', as an irritated Lord Grange complained in a letter to Thomas Hope from London in January 1741. For her friends, it was as though someone had spoken from beyond the grave, so complete had been the silence since her disappearance almost nine years previously.

CHAPTER 22

The Riddle of the Letters

...do me justes and relieve me, I beg you make all hast but if you hear I'm
dead do what you think right befor God.
Letter from St Kilda, 20 January 1738, Lady Grange

I am not sure who of my kin and friends is dead, or who is alive, but I beg
whoso-ever hands this comes first to, to cause write it over in a fair hand and
to shew it to all my friends.
Letter from St Kilda, 21 January 1741, Lady Grange

TEASING OUT THE facts of the two letters from Lady Grange which
finally reached Edinburgh is as difficult and frustrating as trying to
unwind a tangled ball of wool. The analogy comes to mind since one of
the suggested routes by which Lady Grange is said to have smuggled a
letter to the mainland was by hiding it in a 'clue' or ball of yarn.

This is one of the more persistent tales told of Lady Grange, but it
has no basis in reality. The only credible route for her letters to reach
Edinburgh is the obvious one: Roderick MacLennan took both with
him when he left St Kilda in 1739. The January 1741 date on the second
letter confuses the issue, but must have been added later by someone
who made a fair copy of the original of this. The original letter has
unfortunately not survived.

Putting pen to paper must have been difficult, if not impossible, for
Lady Grange in the early years. Her jailers would have made sure she
possessed neither, and both of her letters refer to want of paper and
lack of a good pen. But with the passing of time it seems they may have
become more relaxed.

The 1738 letter, begun six years into her imprisonment, is addressed to

Lady Grange's letter to Charles Erskine, the Solicitor General, dated St Kilda: Jan 20 1738.
It arrived in Edinburgh in December 1740.

Charles Erskine of Tinwald, the Solicitor General for Scotland. It is signed 'your most humble servant but infortunat cousen', for Charles Erskine was not only a leading figure in the Scottish law establishment but was also a kinsman. In fact he was no longer Solicitor General, though she would be unaware of this, as he had become the Lord Advocate in 1737. If anything he was now even more obliged to see the law upheld and justice done within the realm of Scotland.

Lady Grange starts off her letter to Charles Erskine by flattering him, liberally scattering biblical references as she compares him to Job and reminds him of the promises made to those who are the peacemakers. She appeals to him and to Lord Dun to make peace for her with her husband: 'I know he will do much be the advices of friends.' She suggests that if her husband's allies intercede successfully for her release it will prevent the dishonour which will otherwise be left on Lord Grange's memory. But she puts a sting in the tail: 'if friends cannot prevaile with Ld Grange then let me have the Benefit of the law'. Having made that crystal clear, she goes on to give an account of her treatment, from her kidnapping in Edinburgh on 22 January 1732 to her time on St Kilda. She names names and, like her husband, has forgotten and forgiven nothing. Charles Erskine will not be able to complain of lack of evidence for the prosecution. 'You may be sure I have much more to tell then this,' she concludes, advising Erskine that she has also given a much fuller account to the minister in St Kilda, who has written it down. So the greater part of the second letter is already in existence before the first letter is completed.

The second letter reads more like a formal deposition of evidence, beginning as it does with 'I, the unfortunate wife of Mr James Erskine of Grange. That after I had lived near 25 years in great love and peace, he all of a sudden took a dislike to my person, and such a hate that he could not live with me...' There follows the more detailed account that Roderick MacLennan had written down to Lady Grange's dictation. The final part, written in her own hand, is a sad coda to MacLennan's ministry on St Kilda and to the friendship which had grown up between them. The minister had planned a visit to Edinburgh. Though he refused to take the second letter with him he agreed to take some 'bills' with him for three of her friends so that they might know where she was. It was a naïve decision and soon regretted. According to Lady Grange he was hindered from going to Edinburgh and returned to St Kilda fearful for his life.

Afraid to visit Lady Grange himself, he sent his wife to tell her that he had burned the 'bills' she had given him. He begged her to return the account of her abduction so that he might destroy it and so that 'it might never come to light again as written by him'. This Lady Grange was unwilling to do and she dealt with the matter with characteristic resourcefulness. 'Since I could not get paper to write so full an account as this I thought it no sin to deceive her,' she writes, 'and I burnt two papers before her, and bade her tell the minister now to be easy.'

MacLennan's abortive attempt to go to Edinburgh must have been in 1738. The following year, when he left St Kilda never to return, he took the two letters with him. What little space remained at the bottom of the second letter Lady Grange used for some disjointed remarks which are, as it turned out, the last we are ever to hear from her. Written under stress and in a hurry, these final comments have their own poignancy. It is here that we read that any time Sir Alexander Macdonald wrote about her the name he gave her was 'the cargo'. That had bitten deep. Here too she takes a last chance to name guilty parties and suggest witnesses. 'The minister's daughter saw me taken out of Mrs Margaret McLean's house by Roderick McLeod,' she writes, 'and the wife of Alexander Macdonald in the Hesker knows it was Lord Lovat and Roderick McLeod that stole me.' As for Lord Lovat's lies, including that she was going to kill her husband, she pleads her innocence for the last time with a simple 'you know that a lie'.

Would her plea for justice find a hearing in Edinburgh? The confederacy was confident of its ability to deal with any threat Roderick MacLennan might pose. Yet there was one man in the capital who might prove more difficult. He was a lawyer and an advocate, but did not belong to Erskine's circle. He could neither be bullied, nor manipulated. Lord Lovat had called him 'that insolent fellow' in a bad-tempered letter to his cousin Thomas Fraser. In his hands lay Lady Grange's only hope of being rescued and receiving justice. Appropriately enough his name was Hope, Thomas Hope of Rankeillour.

CHAPTER 23

Hope of Rankeillour

She has been so harshly and barbarously used, that I dar say her Husband knows nothing of it, for his friends from him I suppose, always assured me all care was taken of her. I doubt not but she may be dead by this time, but if she is alive, the hardest heart on earth would bleed to hear of her sufferings, and I think I can't in duty stand this call, but must follow out a course so as to restore her to a seeming liberty and a comfortable life.
Letter to Charles Erskine, 13 December 1740, Thomas Hope

It is enough to tell you in general that I was of the opinion as much as you that the lady should have been placed somewhere that she could have given no disturbance to you or your family, but that, at the same tyme, she should not be quite deprived of her liberty and comfortable livelihood, of both which it appears she has been these several years, to the reproach of the country, of Christianity, and all her relations.
Letter to Lord Grange, 23 February 1741, Thomas Hope

THOMAS HOPE WAS not looking for confrontation. He had been party to the original decision to have Lady Grange removed from the family circle and had accepted that her conduct necessitated separation. Assured that she was well cared for, he had been content to let matters rest. Until, that is, early December 1740 when letters were left at his house 'by an unknowen hand'.

Hope lost no time in forwarding the letter addressed to Charles Erskine to the intended recipient, informing him that he himself had received a second letter. This can only be the deposition-style letter, the original of which is now lost. That it would be addressed to Hope, Lady Grange's appointed lawyer, makes perfect sense. A reference to staying in 'your house' for a few months after the separation agreement also points to their close family connection.

While Edinburgh buzzed with the news of the prisoner of St Kilda, Hope still wished to proceed 'with the caution and moderation the Lord Advocate shall direct and Grange and his friends could wish'. So he states in his letter to Erskine. As it happens he is suffering from colic and might or might not be abroad the next day. If he is able, and if Erskine is to be taking tea by himself, then he hopes to have the honour of waiting upon him.

Whether that particular meeting happened is not known but Hope did meet with both Charles Erskine and Lord Dun within a few days of the arrival of the letters. On the agenda for discussion were possible alternatives to avoid the necessity of taking legal action. There was clearly not going to be an immediate rush to rescue Lady Grange or to move against the men she had accused.

The longer any direct action was delayed or process of law blocked, the better it suited the confederates. Above all else, delay would give them time to deal with the main piece of evidence against them. Weather permitting, the 'cargo' could be moved.

All this time Grange was in London. Hope wrote to him on 6 January 1741, but if he expected some support from that quarter he was to be severely disappointed. Grange let two posts go by before replying on 17 January, only to go over old ground, vindicating the removal of his wife by recalling her past behaviour, and attacking Hope personally, and with a particular viciousness, for his supposed part in stirring up trouble in Edinburgh.

Grange's barbs hit home. Replying on 23 February, Hope robustly defends himself against the charge that he did not have the interests of the Erskine family at heart. Far from spreading the story of the unfortunate lady, he had gone in person to the provost's house, when he heard that Lady Grange's letter was to be publicly printed, and got the provost out of bed to send immediately to the printers to have the printing stopped. If he was prompted by malice, then, 'why did I waste the time in writing to you?' Hope asks. 'What hindred me joyning with the opinion of many who were directly for carrying things to the extremity the law allows, and that against all concerned?' Conscience and honour were his only prompters and guide and Grange's reproaches would have no effect on his conduct. 'Those,' Hope tells Grange, 'I altogether despise.'

In this exchange it is striking that Lady Grange is never mentioned by name by either man. Grange refers to her as 'the person' or 'that person'. Hope is kinder, calling her 'the lady', but he never uses her name or alludes to her as Grange's wife. It is as though he knows instinctively that it would not go down well with his correspondent to remind him of a relationship he no longer wishes to acknowledge.

Hope acted with great caution from the start. As he put it in his first letter to Charles Erskine, 'it is a tender affair to be compromised among friends'. Only if that does not prove to be possible would he take 'all legal steps' to relieve Lady Grange. Hope was willing to compromise, but he no doubt anticipated that Lord Grange did not share his wish to see Lady Grange's comfort and liberty restored (with the proviso that she stay well away from her family). Significantly, when he came to write his detailed response to Grange on 23 February, Hope did not mention that he has gone ahead with a plan to search St Kilda and that the sloop *Arabella*, under the command of Captain William Gregory, has left Greenock on its way to the island with more than 20 armed men on board. Also on board was Mrs MacLennan, a Gaelic-speaker whose knowledge of the island and acquaintance with Lady Grange would have been considered a valuable addition to the enterprise. Hope had earlier applied for a warrant from the Lord Justice Clerk to search St Kilda, only to have the application opposed by Grange's friends and eventually refused. So the decision to send the *Arabella* was a bold and unexpected move. But who would challenge its legality if Captain Gregory's mission was successful and he returned with Lady Grange? In the event, of course, that did not happen. The *Arabella* was already too late.

The story of the ship's fruitless voyage is summed up in one leaf of paper held in the Scottish National Archives, a copy made from the original by Lord Medwyn in the 19th century. There we can read the letter Hope gave to Captain Gregory to deliver to the MacLeod laird of St Kilda, and an additional note from Gregory when he sent the letter on by bearer to MacLeod, having failed to find Lady Grange on St Kilda or deliver Hope's letter personally. Finally there is MacLeod's reply, squeezed into what remains of the space. Strangely enough, all three men refer to Lady Grange as 'unfortunate' (an epithet which seems to stick to her like a burr), but how much genuine sympathy that implies is debatable. The words rendered in italics in the text are an educated guess, where the writing is difficult to decipher.

Hope's letter, written from Edinburgh, is dated 14 February 1741:

Sir, In December I received letters from the unfortunate Lady Grange dated att St Kilda, January 1738, describing her miserable condition and praying me to obtain her release. This was communicate to Mr Erskine of Grange att London and some of his friends here, who both exprest their great unwillingness that any application should be made to a Court of Justice for her deliverance by a legal authority; nor indeed was that needful unless she should be detained where she was, or carried somewhere else by force. I therefore have sent the bearer Cpt MacGregory with his sloop *Arabella* in order to bring her away from St Kilda and directed him in case she should not be found there, though still alive, to repair forthwith to you and deliver this. The content of which, in that case, is to entreat the favour of Justice from you, which is certainly in your power, to give the Bearer your protection and assistance to discover where that unfortunate lady is, and to bring her away with him; in which if the bearer should not succeed, there will then remain no other remedy for me to pursue but to trye what force and authority the Law can have in those parts where she has been and shall be so detained. But this I hope you will have the goodness to prevent, from the good Character I hear of you, and for the sake and quiet of all concerned, which I so much wish *and labour for*. I am with all respect, Sir, your most obliged and humble servant – Th. Hope

To this letter Captain Gregory adds his own, written from 'Lorn' on 28 March:

Sir, According to orders and directions from Mr Hope of Rankeillor I went to the Island of St Kilda to enquire for the unfortunate Lady Grange, but being informed that she was removed from that place some time ago and likeways informed of the *place* of her present abode, it being in a place I cannot goe conveniently with my vessel, my next orders were wait upon at

Dunvegan and deliver the inclosed, but being well informed you were not at home I came here *Nr Lorn* where I am obliged to remain till I receive your answer which I humbly intreat by the Bearer himself and according to the answer I shall receive from you must take my *resolutions* according to my instructions from my employer. Yrs Gregory

Finally there is an unsigned letter, dated 3 April, from Inverness, which is clearly from MacLeod. He reveals himself to be an expert in stonewalling:

Sir, My return last night brought me yours of the 28th at Lorne alongst with a letter from Rankillar, wherein you are pleased to tell me you have searched St Kilda for unfortunate Lady Grange, that she is not there, but that you've some information where she is, you'll please on receit of this lett me know the particulars of your information and in what manner I can be of service to you. I shall then be able to judge what is proper for me to do consonant with the *Rules* of Justice and *Humanity Honour*. I am, Sir...

This is the second time in as many months that MacLeod has pled ignorance on the subject of Lady Grange. A warrant signed in the holograph of MacLeod at Dunvegan on 17 February 1741, which is quoted in *Chambers Edinburgh Journal* of 7 March 1846, refers to a rumour which has reached the writer 'that a certain gentlewoman, called Lady Grange, was carried to his isle of St Kilda in 1734 and has ever since been confined there under cruel circumstances'. Regarding this 'as a scandal which he is bound to enquire into', MacLeod orders his baron-bailie of Harris, Donald MacLeod of Berneray, to proceed to the island and make the necessary investigations.

Since this same gentleman had already been to the island the previous October to collect statements on the treatment of Lady Grange, it seems unlikely he would return in March to check on a rumour that she might be imprisoned there. In any case he would know full well, as would the laird of MacLeod, that Lady Grange was no longer on St Kilda. She may indeed have been removed in the late summer of 1740, even before Donald MacLeod went there.

Outplayed in the game of Hunt the Lady in the Hebrides, Thomas

Hope was left to count the cost of the *Arabella* adventure. 'To cash given Mrs MacLennan who went along with Captain Gregory, for getting home her trunk and baggage, £2. 14s.' was just one of the less expensive items. More substantial costs would have to be settled. Any prospect of recouping these, let alone of achieving any kind of justice for Lady Grange, now rested on private negotiations and the outcome of court proceedings.

CHAPTER 24
The Confederates Close Ranks

There is one thing I wish there may be proof of, because all along I have
been informed it is true viz. that that person continued and continues in the
same temper and disposition of fury, passion, and unpersonableness... These
have been and continues to be reasons of confinement which will be a main
point of the future conferences.
Letter to John MacLeod, advocate, 20 April 1741, Lord Grange

THERE IS ONE more illuminating communication from this period in the
National Archives. This is a long, rambling, and unsigned letter to John
MacLeod, Advocate, Edinburgh, dated 20 April 1741, written from
Boroughbridge in Yorkshire. By the tone of the letter, the sycophantic
reference to Lord Lovat and the disparaging comments on 'that person',
it is not difficult to work out the identity of the writer. Lord Grange has
finally left London and is posting his way north. This too is a copy of
the original by Lord Medwyn.

John MacLeod had been writing to Grange, raising various points
on which he would like advice. In reply Grange is confident that all can
be brought to a satisfactory conclusion. The matter has not yet been
brought before the court, but if it does reach that stage, 'her deportment
and disposition will satisfy the publick and courts and make all end
well,' he tells MacLeod.

Sequestration had always been the reason given by Grange for the
forcible removal of his wife. This legal term was used as a justification
for dealing with anyone judged to be of unsound mind who had become
unfit to have the management of his or her family. It explains why Grange
was so set on emphasising the uncontrolled behaviour of his wife. As he
had argued at the time of the separation agreement, there was not at the

time a 'madhouse'. What could a man do with such a wife?

This was obviously still his main argument. It could be countered by Lady Grange's lawyer that his client was not of unsound mind. And even if her 'madness' was proved, either in court or in out-of-court discussion, there was still the manner of her treatment and the place of her confinement to be considered. For this reason the precognition, put together from the statements taken by Donald MacLeod on St Kilda, was of vital importance, and Grange had been sent a copy. He informs John MacLeod in the letter that he has not as yet had time to read the precognition, though he has noticed a reference at the end of it to the wretchedness of the lodging on the island. This had been described as having an earthen floor, with rain and snow coming through the walls and roof, making it necessary to scoop the water out and remove the snow in handfuls from behind the bed.

These few plain facts sound credible, and the only surprise is that such a negative account was not screened out of the precognition. Surely it would also make uncomfortable reading for Lord Grange? Not so, apparently. Grange feels secure enough to dismiss it as a 'pretended account'. Nor does he seem disturbed that he is still ignorant of the particular complaints made by 'that person' in her letters and narratives. He does not doubt that John MacLeod has seen all the letters, precognitions and narratives and he is confident that the evidence on the other side will 'get all in a true light'.

In his letter Grange for some reason refers to Hope as 'the Don' and, in the manner of the period, inserts dashes in place of some of the letters in proper names. He tells John MacLeod that his friend 'Ol—v—b' (Olivestob) had written to him reporting a conversation he had had with the Don who at that time was preparing to hire a sloop and send for that person to 'St K—a'. Ol—v—b had advised the Don that such action was needless since all would be set right on Grange's home-coming. The Don however had insisted he would continue with his course of action. Whereupon Ol—v—b told him that although he had 'nothing of it' from Grange, he had hints from others that 'St K—a was not now the place.'

'Then,' said the Don, 'I'll demand that person from the Laird of Mc—d.'

'He will answer you,' said Ol—v—b, 'that he is not that person's keeper.'

On the laird of MacLeod's unhelpful attitude Olivestob could not have been more prophetic.

There is some confusion over the date when Hope lost patience with the prevarications of Lord Grange and his friends and took legal action on Lady Grange's behalf. According to the Sobieski Stuarts, Hope had already tried and failed to have John MacLeod of Muiravonside answer to the charges of Lady Grange's abduction, even before the *Arabella* set sail from Greenock in February. On the other hand we have this letter from Grange to John MacLeod in April, advising him that the unreasonable behaviour of Lady Grange was the most powerful argument should the matter come to court.

Whatever the order of events, it does seem that John MacLeod of Muiravonside, advocate in Edinburgh, was the person who eventually appeared in court on behalf of his kinsmen and Lord Grange. His defence was that he had no authority to reply for the latter, and for the former he repelled the charges by claiming that no warrant should be issued against them on the evidence of such scandalous and discredited persons as MacLennan and his wife.

Hope was directed by the judges to produce the letters said to have been written by Lady Grange from St Kilda. When these were provided they were dismissed as insufficient evidence, on the grounds that they were not in Lady Grange's handwriting. This must refer to the 1741 letter, the greater part of which was certainly written by MacLennan, but which also included the final section written by Lady Grange.

The legal waters may have been muddied by the many fair copies of this letter which were made, at Lady Grange's request, by those who received it, but the big question which must be asked is why Lady Grange's original 1738 letter, in the possession of Charles Erskine, the Lord Advocate, does not seem to have been produced in evidence. This letter was not only undeniably in Lady Grange's own handwriting, but specifically mentioned that she had given a fuller account of her abduction to the minister, who had written it down at her dictation. This surely would have been sufficient to validate the letter written by MacLennan.

The confederates were of course anxious that the whole business should be decided out of court. 'Noise' was always Lord Grange's bête noire, by which he meant the intrusion of the public into his family's affairs. Jaw-jaw among friends was infinitely preferable to law-law in open court.

The strategy appears to have been successful. At one of these conferences of friends, Lord Grange produced evidence from the St Kilda precognition which absolved him from any wrongdoing. The Sobieski Stuarts name those who attended as Grant, the current Solicitor General, Lord Dun, Mr Robert Craigie of Glendoick, a judge in the Court of Session, John MacLeod, advocate, and Mr Hugh Paterson, Grange's nephew and son to the Baronet of Bannockburn. Hardly an unbiased gathering. 'Upon the testimonies produced,' write the Sobieski Stuarts, 'the auditors declared that Lord Grange had vindicated himself, to which the legal gentlemen added, that if Mr Hope was not also satisfied and still continued his pursuit, they would not appear in his cause.' The Lord Advocate's opinion of these legally dubious cabals is not recorded.

All seems to have been stitched up satisfactorily with no dissenting voices raised. Apart, that is, from the MacLennans, who continued for some time to plead Lady Grange's cause in Edinburgh. Everywhere they went they were met with closed doors and closed minds. They are even said to have approached Lord Grange, who refused to meet them.

Thomas Hope too continued to battle on, if only on the monetary front. Referring back to the separation agreement, when Lady Grange was awarded £100 annually, Hope raised an action in the Court of Session for payment of £1,150, a sizeable sum in these days, which he claimed were arrears of alimony owed by Grange.

There were several grounds for disputing this. For one thing, the agreement was for five years only, and dependent on Lady Grange 'not troubling' her husband. Grange argued that not only had she violated the stipulations of tranquillity on which the agreement was based but that she had thrice refused to receive dividends of the annuity when they were transmitted to her. There was also the question of Lady Grange's maintenance on St Kilda, another grey area on which little information was available. Contributions which Grange might have made would conceivably have to be taken into account in any settlement.

The case finally came to court in November 1743. Lord Grange avoided casting any light on possible contributions to maintenance on St Kilda, or on any other matters either, by being absent from court, and indeed from Edinburgh. In his absence judgment was given against him by default for the full £1,150 due in arrears, but no payments were ever made and the case was left dormant.

Hope took the proceedings no further, at least for the time being. There was after all the not inconsiderable problem that he had no idea of the present whereabouts of the beneficiary of his legal action. Or indeed if she was still alive.

CHAPTER 25
Politics and Pleasure

His first appearance in the House of Commons undeceived his sanguine
friends and silenced him for ever. He chose to make his maiden speech on the
Witches Bill, as it was called; and being learned in daemonologia, with books
on which subject his library was filled, he made a long canting speech that set
the House in a titter of laughter, and convinced Sir Robert that he had no need
of any extra-ordinary armour against this champion of the house of Mar.
Autobiography, Alexander Carlyle

Lord Grange ruined himself in Parliament on his first appearance by a display
of oratory against the proposal to abolish the statutes against witchcraft.
He maintained that witches ought not to be suffered to live, for such was
the injunction of Scripture. For this fanatical harangue he was laughed at by
Walpole, and simply finished himself as a politician.
Chambers Magazine, 14 July 1874, William Chambers

ALL THE YEARS Lady Grange was suffering enforced exile it was business
as usual for Lord Grange. Politics and religion took up much of his time,
as it always had done, and in 1734 he stood for election to Parliament.
His decision was partly fuelled by a desire to lend his weight to the
opposition to Walpole, a minister for whom he had developed an intense
aversion. This dislike was more personal than political, stemming from
Walpole's unhelpful attitude over the situation of the Countess of Mar
and the management of the Mar estates.

Even harder for Grange to forgive was Walpole's refusal to press for
a pardon for the exiled Earl of Mar. Grange had written to the minister
in 1727, assuring him that his brother had repented his actions and
renounced Jacobitism and the cause of the Pretender. The following year
Grange wrote to the Duke of Argyll asking him to encourage Walpole

to speak to the king to grant a pardon to Mar. Even if the duke had felt inclined to oblige – and that was by no means certain – Walpole was too wily a politician to get involved in such a matter. Grange's brother was to die unpardoned in 1732, still in exile in Aachen.

Now that there was no longer any reason to seek the favour of Walpole, Grange felt free to embark on a parliamentary career as part of the anti-Walpole group. Walpole, for his part, sought to stymie his parliamentary career before it had even begun by having a clause added to a Bill, then passing through Parliament to regulate elections in Scotland, which would disqualify judges of the Court of Session from becoming Members of Parliament. This would naturally disqualify Grange.

Archibald Campbell, Lord Ilay, may well have been Walpole's accomplice in the business. Considered by some to be 'the Scottish Walpole', Ilay was the most powerful man in Scotland at the time, and shared Walpole's antipathy to Grange. Ilay had, after all, assisted his brother, the Duke of Argyll, in the defeat of the Earl of Mar's Jacobite army at Sheriffmuir, back in 1715. However much Grange had sought to distance himself from his family's past, the old taint of Jacobitism may have played a part in Ilay's antagonism towards him. Grange dealt with the threat of disqualification by resigning as a judge in the Court of Session, after 27 years' service. He chose to stand for the safe seat of Inverkeithing, reckoning without John Cant, the local town clerk, who was already in the pay of the opposing candidate. Although Grange won a majority of the votes, the town clerk made the return in favour of his opponent. The setback, however, proved temporary. Grange was returned to Parliament for Clackmannanshire that same year – and Cant paid dearly for his false return as Grange pursued him successfully through the courts.

In Parliament Grange took an active part in debates, representing Scottish interests in a variety of issues. In time he became secretary to Frederick, Prince of Wales, a relationship which proved to be to the liking of both parties. When Grange sought re-election in 1741 the prince sent his good wishes for his success. Grange was returned, this time for the Burgh of Inverkeithing and District, which must have given him particular satisfaction.

Although now much in London (and still in thrall to Fanny Lindsay, the handsome Scotchwoman with the Haymarket coffee-house), Grange retained his strong links with Scotland, both in correspondence with friends such as Lord Lovat and by regular visits to Edinburgh and Preston. The esteem in which he was held in his native country was underlined in 1735 when the University of St Andrews conferred the degree of Master of Arts on him. Although Grange would never lack critics, nor escape entirely from the aura of suspicion caused by his Jacobite connections, he was enjoying a brief period of sunshine in his life. Did he ever consider that this Elysian spell might come to an abrupt end? Did he spare a thought in his busy life for the woman, still his wife and mother of his children, imprisoned on St Kilda and make it his business to question the quality of life that was being provided for her? Did he ever fear the consequences of information on her situation leaking out?

It would seem not. Even when the first communication from Lady Grange arrived in Edinburgh in 1740 and became the talk of the town, he was confident that all would be made well by the successful networking of the friends who had handled the business in the past. His untroubled demeanour at such a critical time is captured by Alexander Carlyle. It was the summer of 1741. Lord Lovat had come south to Edinburgh, and was mixing business with pleasure. He had brought with him his younger son Alexander, an untutored savage (according to his father) who required an experienced hand to turn him into an educated gentleman. Who better to take on this task than John Halket, who had tutored Lovat's eldest son, Simon, for two years and was now schoolmaster at Prestonpans? And what better than to turn the occasion into a sociable gathering at Lucky Vint's tavern in that village? Lovat could then play host to his good friend Lord Grange.

The company included the youthful Alexander Carlyle, then a student at the college in Edinburgh. He had apparently been invited along as it was thought he might prove 'useful' to Lovat's son. A good influence perhaps on the untutored savage. There was an edginess to the occasion which Carlyle did not miss. 'What I successfully observed,' he writes, 'was that Grange, without appearing to flatter, was very observant of Lovat, and did everything to please him.' Pleasing Lovat

The Reverend Dr Alexander Carlyle, minister of Inveresk (1722–1805).
Engraving, from a painting by David Martin.

could sometimes be difficult. Grange had organised a piper for the after-dinner entertainment, only to have the unfortunate Geordy Sym dismissed by Lovat as 'only fit to play reels to Grange's oyster-women'. Sym at that time was reckoned the best piper in the country, but nobody argued the point with Lovat.

Then there was the business of the fish course. Lovat had arranged the meal beforehand with the landlady: fresh whiting and the best of claret. His Lordship was insistent on whiting, being very averse to haddock. As the landlady had no whiting she ordered her cook to scrape the telltale St Peter's mark off some haddock before presenting them at table, a subterfuge she had used before with success.

All might have been well if Carlyle, asked by Lovat to pass a whiting, had not innocently pointed out that they had been served haddock, quoting the local saying that 'he that got a haddock for a whiting was not ill off'. A warning wink from Halket made Carlyle re-identify the fish before him. A 'whiting' was passed over to Lovat who sampled it, declared himself pleased with it, and informed the company that he never could eat a haddock all his life.

The claret was unquestioned in its excellence and circulated freely. The arrival of Kate Vint, the attractive, black-eyed daughter of the landlady, further enlivened the proceedings and the afternoon closed with both lordships dancing reels with her. Carlyle, son of the manse, looked on. When he came to record the occasion in later life, he could not help being censorious. He had not been impressed by Lovat, a man whose address 'consisted chiefly in gross flattery and in the due application of money.'

But what he terms the 'convivium' of the day was still not over. Lovat's son had to be delivered to his new lodgings. His landlady, a decent widow of a shipmaster, provided tea for the party and was charmed by Lovat's fair speeches. The Fraser clansmen left for Edinburgh on horseback while the others went on, at Grange's invitation, to Preston House.

So it came about that Carlyle found himself unexpectedly in Grange's library, where his father had spent so many hours detained in theological discussion. The room had once been well stocked with books but by this time all that remained was a large collection on daemonology, which had become Grange's particular study.

Claret, rightly suspected by Carlyle's mother to be the third party at the late-night discussions between Grange and her husband, was once more in evidence: 'a new deluge of excellent claret', together with a fine collection of fruit and biscuits. At ten o'clock the two lords mounted their coach and set off for Edinburgh.

When Grange and Lovat enjoyed this day together, public interest in the fate of Lady Grange, generated by the arrival of her letters, had already begun to wane with the failure of the *Arabella* to find any trace of her. There was nothing to trouble the two gentlemen in the coach as they rolled back to Edinburgh. The plight of Lady Grange in the far-distant Hebrides is unlikely to have disturbed the conscience of either lord. If any woman came to mind, the odds are it would have been Kate Vint.

CHAPTER 26

Hebridean Hide-and-Seek

Lady Grange was immured for a time in the cave of Idrigil in Skye, and
afterwards transferred to Uist, the person having the management of the
boat having beside him a rope, with a running noose at one end, and a heavy
stone at the other, intending, according to his orders, to fix the noose round
the prisoner's neck, and to consign her immediately to the deep, should the
sloop of war come in sight during the passage.
New Statistical Account of Scotland, 1845, Archibald Clerk

ONCE LADY GRANGE had been removed from St Kilda, an alternative had
to be found quickly for her future imprisonment. The obvious choice
was Skye, where she could be kept securely in the MacLeods' home
territory. But in 1741, as luck would have it, Norman MacLeod was
wheeling and dealing in a second, and this time successful attempt, to
enter the Westminster Parliament as representative for Inverness-shire.
The last thing he would want was to run the risk of being outed as the
jailer of another MP's missing wife. It might be best in the meantime
to keep the lady on the move. So although she was hastily taken off
St Kilda, perhaps as early as the autumn of 1740, Lady Grange did
not arrive on Skye until 1742. During the intervening period she was,
according to several later accounts, taken first to a farmhouse in Assynt,
where she passed the winter, then on, possibly to Uist, then to Harris
for seven months, and finally to Waternish on Skye. Uist was reserved
as a possible bolthole, if any danger of discovery threatened.

An intriguing letter of 26 November 1763, held among the Muni-
ments at Dunvegan Castle, adds a little more detail on Lady Grange's
movements. Charles MacSween, the writer of the letter, and Norman
MacLeod of MacLeod had fallen out, and the letter is written in anger.

There is even a hint of blackmail as MacSween invites MacLeod to 'consider with yourself what Guest I brought from Harrish in March 42 or by whose orders I kept her seven months and who wrote me in September 42 to deliver her to Rory MacNeil.' It would appear then that Lady Grange was moved from Harris in March 1742 after a seven-month stay, and delivered to Waternish on Skye in September of the same year to live with the family of Rory MacNeil until her death. She can still not be named but at least 'guest' is more kindly than 'cargo'.

From the Reverend Archibald Clerk, writing in the 1845 in the *New Statistical Account of Scotland,* come some of the more colourful details which crop up in stories of Lady Grange, for which he claims 'authority which deserves regard'. It is here that first mention is made of the sofa under which Lady Grange supposedly hid in order to eavesdrop on one of her husband's conferences with the disaffected Jacobite gentry who frequently met at Preston House. Here too are the first references to a letter from Lady Grange being smuggled out hidden in a ball of yarn, and to a mock funeral being held in Edinburgh.

According to Clerk, she learned to spin on Skye from the poor people among whom she lived. Having managed to acquire writing materials she enclosed a letter in a 'clue' of thread of her own making, which went to the market in Inverness as part of the islanders' annual export of yarn. As a result the Government sent a sloop of war to Skye to search for her, and Lady Grange had to be immured for a time in a cave at Idrigil.

No letter of Lady Grange's from Skye has ever been found, nor is there any evidence of a Government sloop being sent to Skye. Nor indeed does learning to spin sound quite like Lady Grange's style. Even so, there lurks under such stories a core of half-remembered reality. The sloop of war may be a memory of Thomas Hope's *Arabella* which had after all almost gone to Skye, and her letters did arrive in Edinburgh, though well before she was moved to Skye and not in the manner suggested. Clerk's chilling account of the method used to transport Lady Grange to Uist from Skye in a boat equipped with the means to dispose of Lady Grange overboard may also have a basis in fact. Desperate times and the threat of discovery could lead men to put in place desperate solutions. And it may be true that Lady Grange was

The mountain of Suilven in Assynt, the area of the Scottish mainland where Lady Grange is supposed to have been taken after her removal from St Kilda.

confined for a time in a cave at Idrigil Point: her association with the cave is still strong in the folk memory of the island.

The cave today is frequented only by sheep, goats and the occasional visitor intrigued to visit 'Lady Grange's cave', but in Clerk's time it was used by local fishermen who dried their nets, cured their fish, cooked their victuals, and slept on the dry sand of the cave's floor. In earlier times it had provided shelter for a variety of people from hermits to outlaws, to the poorest in the community. There is a rich tradition of cave-dwelling in the west of Scotland, stemming back to the Celtic saints of the 6th century, and no doubt further back still, into prehistory. The cave itself is quite large. From a long, low entrance, under 6 feet in height, it opens out into a semi-circular interior some 60 feet wide and almost eight feet high. It is likely that its existence was known only to the islanders themselves and this, together with its remote location, would make it a natural choice for a hiding-place, should any perceived emergency arise. Pity the poor lady if indeed she was confined there. Even after ten years' experience in a variety of overnight halts and lodgings, Lady Grange would surely have found Idrigil the strangest abode she had yet encountered.

Any perceived emergency would more likely be the result of excessive nervousness on the part of Lady Grange's jailers rather than any real risk. Public concern over her fate had peaked in 1741, but even then it was confined to Edinburgh and mainly to the city's upper classes. By the time she had been transferred to Skye she was yesterday's news.

A few years later more momentous happenings in the Hebrides would obliterate any residual interest in Lady Grange. Two months after her death in Skye in May 1745, Charles Edward Stuart, Bonnie Prince Charlie, landed in Eriskay in a doomed final attempt to restore the Stuarts to the British throne. Scotland was caught up in the fervour, and ultimately the tragedy, of the Second Jacobite Rising. Edinburgh was occupied and there was dancing at Holyrood, although the Castle at the top of the Royal Mile held firm for the Hanoverians. England was invaded and the Highlanders reached Derby before turning back for home and the killing field of Culloden.

Post-Culloden, even St Kilda was searched for the fugitive prince. Three vessels, the *Looe,* the *Furnace* and the *Terror* arrived there on 20 June 1746, and a hundred men were landed. For three days they scoured the island, only to find nothing. If only Lady Grange had not written those letters, had not been moved off the island, had lived a few years longer... perhaps, just perhaps, those searching for a prince might have discovered instead a long-lost lady.

CHAPTER 27

The Final Years

The whole transaction for all concerned in it, is worse than odious, and one cannot but sympathise deeply with the unhappy lady who endured for 15 long years the blackness of despair, and at last died among scenes which, however beautiful, could have brought no ray of hope for her anguished heart in her lonely exile.

The Misty Isle of Skye, JA MacCulloch

After some time she was accorded a certain measure of freedom; but her faculties were now beginning to fail and she was allowed to wander about among the kindly disposed people, a wrecked mind in a restless body, until death put an end to her chequered career in the year 1745.

History of Skye, Alexander Nicolson

LATER WRITERS ARE united in painting a sad picture of Lady Grange on Skye. The Sobieski Stuarts claim that even before she was taken from St Kilda, habitual intoxication had begun to affect her moral and physical health and produced symptoms of approaching imbecility. In Assynt she became enfeebled in body and mind. In Skye she exhibited a restless desire to ramble and was allowed to wander from place to place, maintained by the hospitality and tenderness accorded in the Highlands, as a sacred claim, to the idiot poor. An intriguing corrective is to be found in a letter written on 1 June 1745 by Lord Grange from Westminster on being informed of his wife's death:

I most heartily thank you, my dear friend, for the timely notice you gave me of the death of that person. It would be a ridiculous untruth to pretend grief for it, but as it brings to my mind a train of various things for many years back, it gives me concern. Her retaining wit and facetiousness to the last surprises me. These qualities none found in her, no more than common sense or good nature before she went to these parts, and of the reverse of all which, if she had not been irrecoverably possest, in an extraordinary and insufferable degree, after many years' fruitless endeavours to reclaim her, she had never seen these parts. I long for particulars of her death which, you are pleased to tell me, I am to have by next post.

Norman MacLeod (1705 –1772), 22nd chief of the Clan MacLeod and laird of St Kilda. Chalk drawing by Joseph van Haecken, after a painting by Allan Ramsay.

Wit and facetiousness to the last? It is some comfort to think that Lady Grange, at least in the opinion of one unidentified acquaintance, was not to be classed as one of the idiot poor.

A few documents shed some light on the circumstances of her life on the Isle of Skye. Among the most poignant is a letter to Norman MacLeod from Rory MacNeill, the man who had been given the responsibility of having Lady Grange to live in his home. The letter, dated 12 May 1745, is from Trumpan in Waternish. 'These are to inform you,' MacNeill writes, 'that the first in this Familie departed this life about 3 of the Cloak fryday last being the tenth instant.' Her death had put him 'to no small trouble in thir hard times', and he was worried that he would not be able to get any sort of eatables to buy. 'Yet I will doe in it what I can,' he assures MacLeod, 'and seeing you left me no written orders where or how to burie her in caice she should happen to die in this house I hope to see her decently interred Wednesday nixt.' As indeed he did.

Two bills, presented to MacLeod by MacNeill, also survive and copies are reproduced in JA MacCulloch's book *The Misty Isle of Skye*. The first, dated 2 August 1744, shows the cost of Lady Grange's board for a year as £30, with additional necessaries accounting for a further £3 and eleven and a half pence. The second, dated 16 August 1745, lists Lady Grange's board, for nine months only, at £22 and ten shillings, with the expense of her interment at £30. 15s. and 5p.

So Norman MacLeod was the local contact who settled the bills for Lady Grange's board and lodgings on Skye, presumably to be reimbursed later by Grange. It was a small amount, especially in comparison to the £100 annual payment that had been agreed in the separation document. But that belonged to another life, and to another world.

The bills also disprove the claim, which has sometimes been made, that Lady Grange lived on Skye on the charity of the islanders. And if the interment might seem unduly expensive, it should be remembered that she was accorded the luxury of two funerals.

CHAPTER 28
Journey's End

Lady Grange continues to elude us even in death for a parish Elder responsible for raising her only headstone in the 1880s had to set this over the grave of his father as the position of her resting place could not be precisely located.
History of Skye, Alexander Nicolson

AWKWARD TO THE LAST, Lady Grange died when Norman MacLeod was once more preparing for a parliamentary election. Her funeral took place in secret at Trumpan, where she was buried in the churchyard, a few feet, according to one account, from the north wall of the old church. A second funeral was held at Duirinish churchyard, near Dunvegan, where a large company of people were invited to witness the burial of a second coffin, this one filled with turf and stones. No headstone marks either grave. The reason for holding a second funeral remains unclear. Perhaps it was simply to draw any unwelcome attention away from the real funeral. It is hard to imagine a churchyard more fitting than Trumpan for the last resting-place of a woman whose life had begun and ended in tragedy. At its centre is the roofless ruin of the old church, Cille Conain, dedicated to the 7th century St Conan, Bishop of the Southern Isles, and the scene for what has been described as one of the bloodiest episodes in Scottish history. The story is told on the information board outside the gate to the graveyard. Locals question some of the details, but the essentials are undisputed.

In the winter of 1577 the MacLeods of Dunvegan had trapped and suffocated a large number of Macdonalds in St Francis Cave on the island of Eigg, by lighting a fire in the cave entrance. Clanranald, chief of

The stone erected in the 19th century for Lady Grange in Trumpan graveyard on Skye, just outside the walls of the ruined church of Cille Conain.

the Macdonalds of Uist, plotted revenge, and on the first Sunday in May 1578 came calling to Trumpan. Having beached their boats at Ardmore Bay, the Macdonalds surrounded the church, which was packed with worshippers, barred the only entrance, and set fire to the thatched roof. Only one member of the congregation was able to escape – a girl who was pushed through the small window managed to raise the alarm at Dunvegan, although one of her breasts had been severed.

The MacLeod's Fairy Flag was waved and the clansmen set off in pursuit of the Macdonalds. A third tragedy ensued when the Macdonalds, fleeing back to their boats, found that the receding tide had left them high and dry. The MacLeods, showing no mercy, slaughtered them all, burying the bodies in a dyke. The battle is remembered as 'the spoiling of the dyke'.

Lady Grange's burial in the old churchyard was not acknowledged until a church elder on the island arranged in the 1880s to have a stone erected to her memory. By then there was no one to tell the precise location of the grave, so the stone was erected over the grave of the elder's father. Well might Alexander Nicolson, the Skye historian, comment, 'Lady Grange continues to elude us even in death.' The plain stone is so lichened over that it is difficult to read. By searching out the letters, it is finally possible to decipher the inscription.

R.I.P.

RACHEL

WIFE OF

THE HON JAMES ERSKINE

LORD GRANGE

DIED A.D. 1745

No beloved wife, no dear mother of those infants who predeceased her or of those children who outlived her, no maiden name, no record of her date of birth nor of her age, no Sacred to the Memory. Only with the 'R.I.P.' is there a touch of compassion. How different Rachel's tombstone might have been in Edinburgh, if only she had been content to be the douce, forgiving wife.

There is another, much older, stone in Trumpan graveyard to be found not far from the Grange stone. It is a small standing stone with a hole in it, known as the 'trial stone'. Witnesses about to give evidence in a trial would, according to local tradition, be brought to Trumpan, set before the trial stone, blindfolded, and turned around. If they could then place their finger in the hole without touching any other part of the stone itself their testimony could be believed. Since the hole is not much wider than a fingerbreadth, this may just be the Highland way of illustrating how difficult it is to get to the truth about anything.

If only we could summon to Trumpan all those who over the years have provided evidence and stood in judgment on Lady Grange. If we could subject them to the test, it is intriguing to conjecture just how many of them would in fact turn out to be believable.

CHAPTER 29
In Search of the Truth

I have no intention to enter into any investigation of Lady Grange's case.
David Laing, June 1874

WITH THE PROVISO that we shall never have a final verdict based on all the facts and acknowledging that we are dealing with human emotions conveyed to us only through those documents which have survived, it is a temptation not to be resisted to set out what we have on the table and make some kind of assessment. And what immediately becomes apparent is the absence of any female voices, apart from Lady Grange herself. Lord Grange had his friends and admirers, very able and willing to put their opinions down on paper, but there are no women's voices raised either to defend or defame Lady Grange. How interesting it would be to know what Lady Grange's sister, wife of James Hamilton of Olivestob, thought of her brother-in-law. Thomas Hope makes a passing reference to her in his February 1741 letter to Grange, where he mentions that Lady Olivestob had been one of the first to come to his house for a copy of Lady Grange's letter from St Kilda. So we know she was concerned, but where did her sympathies lie?

Or what of Lady Jean, James Erskine's sister? Which of the Granges did she think was the more culpable in the marriage break-up which landed her with the responsibility of the younger children? Or Mary Erskine, Lady Grange's daughter? If only she had put down her thoughts on the mother who was so proud of her fine marriage. Or if Mrs MacLennan had left some written account of the woman she befriended on St Kilda and of the failed attempts to rescue her.

It is more than likely these women would have lined up behind their husbands who, with the exception of the minister, were very much in sympathy with Lord Grange. Still we will never know for sure, and the picture we have of Lady Grange from contemporary witnesses is drawn from an exclusively masculine viewpoint.

Robert Wodrow, an early and enthusiastic apologist for Grange, reckoned him to be 'amongst the greatest men in this time'. Wodrow was influenced and at least partially blinded by his admiration for Grange's involvement in church affairs and religious debate. Reporting on the recent separation of the Granges in his *Analecta* for July 1730, he tells us approvingly that Lord Grange 'did not use any endeavours' to have his wife back, 'since sometimes she attempted to murder him, and was innumerable ways uneasy'. Aware that Lady Grange had charged her husband with 'guilt with another', he has nothing condemnatory to say on this subject. He is more interested in telling us of her drunkenness and her temper. Perhaps he knew nothing of Lord Grange's taste for claret and oyster-women. Or could it be a double standard in operation, making allowances for the husband's drunkenness and immorality, yet requiring a meek and mild demeanour in the wife.

Alexander Carlyle was more even-handed in his judgment and characteristically sharp in his opinion. Grange he considered to be a man of neither learning nor ability, who had been raised on the shoulders of his brother, the Earl of Mar but had never distinguished himself. As for Lady Grange, her outward appearance was 'stormy and outrageous', but Carlyle adds, 'Lord Grange not improbably exaggerated the violence of her behaviour to his familiar friends as an apology for what he afterwards did.'

Lord Lovat was Lord Grange's most enthusiastic supporter, at least on paper. In a letter of 12 October 1736, Lovat assures him that he considers him 'a man of the most singular merit that Scotland had produced in the present age', and one to whom he felt 'most tied in intimate friendship and comradeship'. Grange had recently written to Lovat and his letter had apparently contained 'more religion, divinity, and just politics, as well as more discoveries of the weakness, inconstancy, and ingratitude of man than a hundred volumes that were printed and sold at a high price on those subjects... I keep it in my strong box and will leave it and recommend it to my children.'

Lady Grange lacked such contemporary champions. Even Thomas Hope was circumspect in challenging her husband over the inhumanity of her treatment or his claims of her unacceptable behaviour. Grange destroyed his wife's character so successfully that she has never shaken off the image of an unbalanced termagant.

Maidment conceded that Grange in his lifetime was regarded by some as an insincere double-dealer. In his Preface to Grange's diary he quotes this contemporary rhyme written by 'a lover of truth' in response to an elegy on the death of Colonel Charteris, which had described Charteris as 'the greatest hypocrite'.

> Th' Answer I'll give thee in these few lines
> Perhaps you may think strange,
> In villainy, that he's outshined
> By Hypocret Lord Grange.
> All Charters' sins were open done
> In face of men and skyes
> But Grange kidnapt his wife by noon
> And whoors with upcast eyes.
> Let Charters then rest in his grave,
> He has received his doom;
> He has no place 'mong hypocrites
> That's held till Lord Grange come.

However, Maidment clearly respected Grange and believed that retrospective sympathy for Lady Grange was misplaced and fails to take into account the period and the circumstances. In his judgement, these factors rendered the measure indispensable, albeit illegal. 'Conceive the situation of a man,' he argues, 'whose fortune, if not his existence, was dependent on the caprice of a fickle, ill-tempered female, who to her original natural infirmity added the artificial one of inebriety.' Swayed by Grange's candour in admitting his faults and by his regrets, Maidment had no hesitation in coming to his final conclusion. Lord Grange, for a North Briton of the reign of Queen Anne, was a passably honest gentleman. Lady Grange was an uncontrolled, and therefore dangerous, female with a bad temper and a drink problem.

In David Laing's judgment, Grange was a singular compound of good and bad qualities: an acute and accomplished lawyer, although profligate in his private life. With great pretensions to piety he was restless and intriguing in political affairs, and despite all his manoeuvring he was signally disappointed in his ambitious schemes. Lady Grange, on the other hand, was said by all parties to have been jealous of her husband's irregularities, to be of a fierce, vengeful temper, and a victim of intemperance. 'Such reports,' Laing concludes, 'may not have been wholly unfounded, although much exaggerated.'

Laing, like Maidment, comes down on the husband's side, whose faults they believe to be outweighed by the wife's temper and her addiction to the demon drink; 'jealous of her husband's irregularities', as Laing phrases it, is a typical Victorian fudge – he preferred not to say the word adultery out loud. Yet at the heart of the Granges' tragedy was the age-old problem of three in a marriage. Lady Grange's 'madness' had its roots in her husband's long-term relationship with Fanny Lindsay.

Should we accept Grange's claim that he had a mad wife who required to be sequestrated? Lady Grange's letters do not read like the letters of a mad woman. Of course she is devious, bending the facts to suit her purpose, omitting what she prefers not to remember, and even lying, as when she claims that she did not subscribe to a separation. But if Lady Grange had continued to be emotionally disturbed to the point of 'madness' she would never have survived as long as she did. St Kilda, with its high cliffs and dangerous cliff-top paths, was an open invitation to self-destruction. Even though her life must have seemed at times unendurable, she still wanted to live, and to communicate back to her friends.

If there had been no Fanny Lindsay and no Jacobite conspiracy, Lord and Lady Grange might well have led an unremarked life. If there had been only one of these factors, the tragedy of the Granges might still have been avoided. A mistress and a flirtation with a possible Stuart restoration were, singly, manageable. It was the concurrence of the two together that led on to disaster. Both Granges sought to use Jacobitism for their own ends. Rachel was trying to force James to give up his London mistress by threatening to uncover his Jacobite connections. James sought to be rid of his increasingly difficult wife by presenting her as a potential danger to his Jacobite friends.

Lady Grange could not have realised quite how powerful and ruthless the people were whose personal safety she was endangering. Faced with the distinct possibility of losing their heads, Grange's friends had no compunction in removing her to the far edge of the Gaelic west, where they felt confident of controlling her and where her only release would be through death.

When Lady Grange's second letter from St Kilda first appeared in print in 1817 in the *Edinburgh Magazine,* the gentleman who provided the copy for publication contributed a preface under the name of 'Gael' in which he describes her as 'a victim of the barbarous times in which she lived'. Indeed she was.

Epilogue

Thro a long life of Cunning passed
Old Simon Thou art caught at last
Puzzle you may your Brains with Schemes
Your Wiles will prove but idle Dreams
So the sly Fox that steals the Lamb
With neither Grace, nor Fear, nor Shame
When once he's trapped in griping Gin
He knows he'll suffer for his Sin
Contemporary rhyme

AFTER A TRIAL in Westminster Hall, London, which lasted from 9–19 March 1747, Simon Fraser, Lord Lovat – Lady Grange's old enemy – was found guilty of High Treason and Rebellion for his part in the Second Jacobite Rising. On Thursday 9 April, in his 80th year, he was executed on Tower Green, the last person to be beheaded there.

Not all the members of the confederacy in fact took part in the Second Jacobite Rising. There is no evidence that Roderick MacLeod was actively involved, though his son remembered his father travelling from Edinburgh to London on horseback to make representations on behalf of Jacobites imprisoned there.

John MacLeod of Muiravonside likewise avoided implication. However his only son, Alexander, joined the prince and was sent to Skye to try to persuade the MacLeod clan chief and Sir James Macdonald of Sleat to join the Rising. There was little chance of his mission being successful: both clan chiefs were dismayed that the young prince had arrived with so few men and so little back-up. Even Lovat would be a reluctant rebel, and MacLeod, ever the pragmatist, quickly decided against supporting the venture. His letter to Duncan Forbes of Culloden, reporting

Simon Fraser, Lord Lovat (c.1667– 1747), sketched by William Hogarth when Lovat was imprisoned in London awaiting execution for High Treason and Rebellion.

the arrival of the prince and the paucity of his support, was the first to alert the Government to the Jacobite danger.

Grange, mindful of the personal tragedy that had befallen his brother, was certainly not going to get caught up in such a chancy, ill-prepared affair. Though the early Jacobite victory of Prestonpans was fought just outside the edge of his estate he was not persuaded to change his mind.

In December 1745 Grange married his mistress in London and took her north to Preston House. Carlyle, his ear as always attuned to local gossip, reports that the neighbours refused to call and Fanny soon persuaded James to return to London. There they lived in lodgings in Haymarket with a Government pension of £200 until James's death in January 1754 in his 75th year. Three sons and two daughters from his first marriage survived him.

Grange sold his Preston estate in 1752, partly to Watson's Hospital and partly to his factor, William Ramsay. Preston House itself was replaced in 1832 by a new house in the old English style, built within the park at a cost of nearly £3,000. Some surviving estate walls and an old doo'cot are probably the only traces that remain today from the time of the Granges. Their battle rumbled on in the law courts even after Lady Grange's death. Although Hope had won judgment in 1743 against Lord Grange for £1,150 for unpaid alimony, no payment had ever been made. The death of Lady Grange revived the issue as she had disinherited her children soon after her separation, naming instead as beneficiaries Mrs Thomas Hope and her three daughters, Margaret, Agnes, and Helen.

Hope took up the issue again, this time on behalf of his family. According to the account of the court proceedings in *Chambers Edinburgh Journal* for March 1846, an action was raised for the £1,150 formerly awarded, plus an additional three years of Lady Grange's annuity. For this sum a compound decreet was obtained, which was followed by steps to force payment.

However the Hopes were apparently aware of the dubious nature of this claim, as Grange had substituted an actual subsistence since 1732 in place of the payment of an annuity. They therefore intimated that they had no wish to derive any personal benefit from Lady Grange's bequest and the matter was resolved by Grange agreeing to reimburse Hope for all the expenses he had incurred on behalf of Lady Grange, including those for the sloop which had been hired to proceed to St Kilda for her rescue.

This account is broadly corroborated by the Sobieski Stuarts, who date the 'termination of hostilities' to 24 April 1751. Grange had agreed to the settlement 'in consideration for his children and his family and to relieve them from a litigation which kept alive the memory of their mother's disgrace'. This was in marked contrast to Lady Grange who had, as they do not fail to point out, executed an 'unnatural' will disinheriting all her children, even though the youngest would then have been almost infants and could never have given her serious offence. As always with the Sobieski Stuarts, Lady Grange is the villain.

Hope lived on in Edinburgh and in May 1761 applied to the king for a small pension. By this time he was 81 years old, living in relative poverty with his three daughters in his house in Hopepark in the south of the town, and dependent on a small annuity from his son. His credentials to qualify for a Government pension are set out in a 'Memorial to the King', which provides a much fuller picture of the man who once fought Lady Grange's corner. He had become an advocate in 1701 and

MARGARET MACAULAY

practised at the Bar till 1715. Thereafter 'he never put on the Goun', for he was much more interested in the subject of land improvement than in law. Hope, whose estate of Rankeillour was a few miles from Cupar, had been one of the four members from Fife elected to the old Scottish Parliament, and had at every opportunity voted against the proposed union with the Parliament in London. In 1719 he moved to Edinburgh to better the education of his children. There he became the driving force behind the setting up of an agricultural society, the new enthusiasm of the age, which soon attracted a membership of 350 from the ranks of the nobility and gentry. He also proposed a scheme to the Lord Provost and magistrates, as proprietors, to turn the boggy area of the Borough Loch in the south of Edinburgh into a public park. In 1722 he was successful in obtaining a lease of the area for 57 years at an annual rent of 800 pounds Scots.

Work had already begun to drain the Borough Loch and, with Hope's enthusiastic support, the drainage was completed and plans for the park drawn up. The aim was to create within the park a 24-foot wide walkway, enclosed by a hedge and row of trees on each side. A second walkway, running from north to south, was also envisaged with a hedge and lime-trees and a narrow canal on either side. The suggested names for the new park were Hope's Park or The Meadows. Middle Meadow Walk was opened in 1743.

Twice Hope attempted to escape back to his ancestral home in Fife to spend his retirement improving his own farm. Each time he was summoned back, his presence considered essential for the success of both the Agricultural Society and the Hopepark Trust which had been formed to manage the new park. Eventually he 'flitted bag and baggage' back to Edinburgh, turning over his profitable farm to his son, and working for the next 20 years without fee or reward for the Society and the Trust. Hope had, according to the Memorial, 'wasted his Estate upon the good of his country'. He died in 1771 at the age of 91. Whether he succeeded in his application for a pension is not known but, more lasting than any pension, is the legacy he left to his adopted city. The Meadows remain to this day a much loved and much used public green space and Hope himself is remembered still in street names in the area.

162

For Roderick MacLennan, Lady Grange's other male champion, a less happy fate awaited. He never did recover from the ill-luck of coinciding with her on St Kilda. When he and his wife arrived in Edinburgh in 1740 they were ostracised and condemned as immoral rogues from the evidence taken against them on St Kilda. In June 1742 he was called before the SSPCK committee, where he denied all the charges against him, dismissing them as vicious and invalid, and made in his absence. Since the charges were based less on the need for a balanced appraisal of the St Kilda minister and more on the necessity to invalidate any evidence the MacLennans might attempt to give on the treatment of Lady Grange, he might well have had a point. The SSPCK committee, however, were unconvinced and withdrew their support from him without actually investigating the matter further.

Somehow MacLennan was able to find alternative employment with the Royal Bounty Commission and in 1743 appeared in Sutherland as an itinerant missionary for the Committee for the Reformation of the Highlands, with a salary of £20 a year, not much less than his St Kildan income had been. Perhaps a combination of his knowledge of the 'Irish language', still much in use in the north of Scotland, together with the clout of being an ordained Church of Scotland minister, helped in his appointment. Edinburgh, never mind St Kilda, was far enough away to allow MacLennan to make a fresh start in the north. Unfortunately this did not happen. His career in various posts in Sutherland and Caithness continued on a downward spiral. Presbytery reports on the quality of his work were uneven and sometimes downright hostile. He failed to find or retain the support of colleagues.

It may have been, as Robson suggests, that 'certain members of the Caithness Presbytery were heavily prejudiced against MacLennan whatever he did'. By 1746 he had been shunted off to the remote island of Stroma in the Pentland Firth off the coast of Caithness. There he remained as catechist and schoolmaster, employed once more by the SSPCK, till his death, probably in 1757, when a decision had already been taken to terminate his employment. MacLennan's final years were plagued by poverty and ill-health. No help was to be found from an unsympathetic Presbytery of Caithness within whose bounds he laboured. Indeed when the presbytery was informed by the SSPCK of the decision to dismiss him and that a replacement had been appointed, there was a distinct lack of Christian charity in the tone of their response: 'We cannot but inform the Society anent Mr McLennan's Case that he is still bad and disordered in his mind,' the presbytery replied. 'He has been long in the Service, and will in all probability in a short time hence be in a miserable Condition, destitute of bread for himself and his Family.'

Ironically MacLennan's final years were spent on an island very reminiscent of St Kilda. The inhabitants of Stroma were poor, their poverty made worse by the severity of the work demanded of them – not unlike the steward's demands on St Kilda. Children could not be spared by their parents to attend school, and poor attendance became another stick with which to beat the schoolmaster. Communication between the island and the Scottish mainland was as difficult as any he had experienced on St Kilda.

Both islands would struggle to retain their native populations and in the 20th century both would admit defeat. In August 1930 the last residents would be evacuated from St Kilda at their own request. Stroma survived a little longer but by 1962 the last two families had left. Apart from short visits by a Caithness farmer to see to the resident sheep and by the lighthouse service to check on the island's automated lighthouse, Stroma remains deserted. St Kilda, on the other hand, has re-entered the world in a different and unexpected way.

As for the Erskine family, in 1740 a marriage occurred which would have unexpected consequences for both Lord and Lady Grange. In that year their son James Erskine married his full cousin, Lady Frances Erskine, only daughter of the attaindered Earl of Mar and his second wife, Lady Frances Pierrepoint. Lady Grange in the Outer Hebrides would have known nothing of this marriage but it was an important one with consequences for her descendants. When Thomas, Lord Erskine, the only son and heir of the exiled earl and half-brother to Frances, died in 1766 without issue, ownership of the largely-restored Mar estates, together with the claim to the Mar title, passed to James and Frances. Their son, John Francis Erskine, had the attainder on the Mar title reversed in his favour on 17 June 1824, the year before he died.

John Francis Erskine, grandson of Lord and Lady Grange, in the grounds of Alloa House with his family. He became the 7th Earl of Mar in 1824, when the earldom was restored to the Erskine family. Rachel, daughter of Lord and Lady Grange, is seated centre. Painted by David Allan, 1783.

The long struggle to have the Earl of Mar title restored to the Erskine family had finally come to a successful conclusion in the person of the grandson of Lord and Lady Grange. Both would have been delighted. In this regard at least, the story of James Erskine and Rachel Chiesley had a happy ending.

Appendices

The Family Register
from Lord Grange's Spiritual Diary

THE ORIGINAL DOCUMENT used by Maidment to produce *Extracts from the Diary of a Senator of the College of Justice 1717–18* is held in the Scottish National Archives in General Register House in Edinburgh. There it is described as 'Grange's Spiritual Diary', though the hand-written title on the front cover is 'Memoirs VII from 13 October 1717 till 5 November 1718'. It is similar in binding and in the religiosity of its content to the 'Memoirs of Lord Grange for the year 1726' which is held in the National Library of Scotland. Both memoirs, handwritten in ink, with occasional blobs as the nib is recharged, are soul-searching documents making only occasional reference to worldly matters. But the memoir in the National Archives has an additional treasure hidden inside its front cover. There in Lord Grange's writing, is a list of his family's births and deaths.

Birth of myself	12 October 1679
Wife	
Charlie	27 August 1709
Johnie 26 March	1711
Jammie 6 March	1713
Mary 5 July	1714
Meggie 4 December	1715
Fannie 14 December	1716
Jeannie 5 December	1717
The death of Johnie	13 May 1711
The death of Meggie	22 May 1717

His daughter Rachel and a second John were yet to be born. In addition Lady Grange had two miscarriages at the start of the marriage: Mary, Countess of Mar, refers to poor Rachel 'miscarrying again' in a letter of condolence to her son James in April 1708. In 1721 Allan Logan, minister of Culross, wrote to express his sympathy to Lord Grange over the death of one of Grange's children. The tally would therefore seem to be nine children born, three early deaths, and two known miscarriages. Why Lord Grange failed to fill in a date for his wife's birthday is anyone's guess.

Law and Marriage

LOCAL COMMISSARY COURTS and a central court in Edinburgh to deal with actions of divorce, separation, and nullity were established in Scotland in the 1560s. Initially considered spiritual in their authority, they were gradually secularised but even from their inception the Court of Session, Scotland's supreme civil court, exercised a supervisory jurisdiction. The Commissary Court in Edinburgh survived as late as 1830, when its functions were taken over entirely by the Court of Session.

There was even a Scottish equivalent to legal aid. Lady Grange, had she so desired, could have applied for this. She would then have had to be placed on the poor roll and a certificate sought, signed by the ministers and elders of her parish, affirming her poverty-stricken state. 'Solicitors for the poor' would have to be satisfied that her case was genuine. Applications were rarely refused, but equally rarely made. Although Lady Grange complained bitterly enough to her family of lack of money, a public admission of her penury might well have been a different matter.

Lady Grange could have raised an action for adultery against her husband. Scottish divorce law made simple adultery equal grounds for divorce for men and women. This was fundamentally different from the law in England where a single act of adultery by the wife was an unpardonable breach of the law of property and hereditary descent, while adultery by the husband was generally regarded as a regrettable but understandable foible. As Leah Leneman points out in *Alienated Affections: The Scottish Experience of Divorce and Separation 1684–1830*, in Scotland in the latter half of the 18th century, 'nearly half of the divorce petitions came from wives who certainly did not regard their husband's extra-marital activities as a regrettable and understandable foible'.

In the 1730s an action for divorce was a protracted business. It entailed engaging lawyers: a 'procurator' licensed to plead before the commissary court and an agent to carry out the investigations and do all the paperwork. A libel had to be drawn up, followed by a summons to be delivered to the defendant's house, calling on him or her to appear in court for the first hearing two weeks later. If the defendant's residence was unknown and/or he or she was believed to be out of Scotland, then the messenger could call out the summons at three specific locations – the market square of Edinburgh and the pier and shore of Leith – and a longer period was granted before the first hearing.

If, after all this, the defendant failed to appear then the action continued in his or her absence. The pursuer would have to swear a solemn oath that their spouse was guilty of adultery and that there was no collusion between them. The pursuer would then go on to give proof for the action for adultery. If the commissaries (judges) were convinced of the validity of the case, divorce was granted, the guilty party was declared legally dead, and the innocent party was entitled to everything that would have come to him or her on the death of the spouse.

For a woman this would normally mean a third of her husband's moveable estate and a third of a life-rent of his heritable estate if there were children from the marriage. If there were no children she was entitled to one half of the moveable estate as well as the third of the life rent. The innocent party was free to marry anyone. The guilty party could also remarry, though not to the person named in the adultery action. Successful women pursuers could also claim the expenses of the case.

If only Lady Grange could have been sure of a successful outcome, this course of action had much to recommend it. How satisfactory to have a substantial financial settlement and to dish the hopes of the Haymarket coffee-house owner of becoming the second Lady Grange.

But would she have been able to prove adultery? And Lord Grange had so many powerful friends, especially in the church and the judiciary. Divorce actions were still rare occurrences. For the period 1731–40 only ten divorces were recorded by the Commissary Court and until 1770 they averaged only one or two a year.

Separations before the Commissary Court were as rare as divorces, but there the courts had the power to decide the amount of aliment (alimony) based on a statement of the husband's financial circumstances which the wife was required to provide. The court also set the dates on which aliment was to be paid. Informal separation agreements, after discussion between the family and friends of both parties, were much more common. It was probably, in the circumstances, the most that Lady Grange could expect.

The Sobieski Stuart Brothers

JOHN SOBIESKI STOLBERG STUART and Charles Edward Stuart arrived in Scotland in the 1820s, and in the 1840s began to claim publicly that they were the legitimate grandsons of King Charles III (Bonnie Prince Charlie). The elder brother used the title Count d'Albanie until his death when his brother Charles took it on. They claimed that their father had been born in 1773 to Queen Louise of Stolberg and King Charles and had been handed over as a baby to the captain of an English frigate for safe-keeping, for fear he might be assassinated by the Hanoverians. They offered no real evidence for this wild claim but were welcomed and taken up enthusiastically by several members of Scottish society, including the 14th Lord Lovat who is said to have built a villa for them on an island in the Beauly Firth. They seem to have chimed in with the contemporary interest in the romanticised Scot and the brothers always wore Highland dress of kilt and belted plaid. In 1841 they wrote *Tales of the Century: Sketches of the Romance of History between the years 1746 and 1846.*

Elizabeth Grant of Rothiemurchus writes amusingly of them in her *Memoirs of a Highland Lady*: 'they one day announced they were Stuarts, lineally descended from Prince Charles… Nobody was more astonished at this assumption than their own father, a decent man who held some small situation in the Tower of London.'

Intensely Jacobite in their sympathies, the brothers rarely miss an opportunity to blacken Lady Grange's character. Collected some hundred years after the events described, their stories should be handled with care. But it should also be remembered that they were given to them by those whose ancestors might well have been involved in the abduction of Lady Grange and that they provide useful information from the Jacobite side.

Some Variations on the Theme of Lady Grange

PUBLIC INTEREST IN Lady Grange was first revived by Dr Johnson's passing reference to her in Boswell's *Journal of a Tour to the Hebrides (1785)*. Her story inspired 'Epistle from Lady Grange to Edward D— Esq', which falsely announced itself to have been written by her 'during her confinement in St Kilda'. An instant success when it appeared in 1798, it is attributed to a young Edinburgh advocate, William Erskine. Lady Grange was back in the news. Presenting her sad fate as punishment for an adulterous love affair, the poem taps into the contemporary taste for romanticism, as the following excerpts show:

> The simple maid, whose thoughts, devoid of guile,
> Ne'er pass'd the limits of the sea-girt isle,
> In ev'ry trouble finds a sure relief
> For mild Religion soothes her rising grief.
> Does cold Disease slow waste her fading bloom?
> Hope cheers her soul, and points beyond the tomb.
>
> * * *
>
> But me – nor Heaven, nor smiling Hope can cheer;
> Wrapt in dark mists my future paths appear;
> Bright to my view the scenes of child-hood rise,
> But gnawing Conscience blasts their brilliant dyes...

Almost 40 years after its publication, James Maidment dismisses the poem as 'wretched trash' and attacks its author for not being 'a matter of fact personage'. He also refutes the suggestion that Lady Grange had been detected in an affair, with the dismissive observation that she was old and ugly when she was carried off.

Among other writings inspired by her story is WC MacKenzie's *The Lady of Hirta, a Tale of the Isles* (1905), a rattling good yarn which purports to be the narrative of the Reverend Ferchard Ross, missionary to St Kilda, who attempts to gain justice for Lady Grange. *Historical Memoirs of Rob Roy and the Clan Macgregor* by Kenneth Macleay MD, published in 1818, includes a section entitled 'Original Notices of Lady Grange'.

Macleay's sources were, he claims, both written and oral, and principally collected during a journey through Skye. He felt, like 'Gael' before him, that Lady Grange had been a victim of the spirit of the times.

Sue Glover's two-act play, *The Straw Chair*, is set on Hirta during one summer between 1735 and 1740. First performed in Edinburgh in 1988, it chronicles the interplay between Lady Grange, her St Kildan servant Oona, the visiting minister Aeneas Seton and his young bride, Isabel. Lady Grange is by turns mischievous and melodramatic, someone to be pitied but also to be carefully watched. The Setons are overwhelmed by the problems she brings to them. Oona is secure in her own culture. Their imagined conversations perhaps come as close as we are likely to get in fiction to poor Lady Grange's actual situation on St Kilda.

St Kilda – A Changing Island

ON 29 AUGUST 1930 the remaining population of St Kilda, numbering only 36 adults and children, were taken off the island at their own request, bringing to an end, for the time being, a long history of human occupation. It was not a decision taken lightly, but the stress of living on the edge of the world had become insupportable. Only two native-born St Kildans still survive, at time of writing.

Norman John Gillies, born in 1925, spent the first five years of his life at Number Ten Village Bay. His clear memories of these early days have been used as commentary to films of island life and with the recent upsurge of interest in St Kilda he has taken part in stage presentations with a backdrop of old and new films of St Kilda, taking the story of St Kilda all over the country, as far south as the Barbican in London. It was the death of his 36-year-old mother, Mary, which proved the tipping point for the community debate about evacuation. Bad weather prevented her from seeking medical care on the mainland and though she did finally reach hospital in Glasgow, she died on 26 May 1930 from appendicitis. Her newborn baby, Annie, also died.

The following year there was another seismic change, as the MacLeod family, so long the island's lairds, sold St Kilda to the Earl of Dumfries, later 5th Marquis of Bute. The island group was managed as a bird sanctuary until the marquis's death in 1956, when St Kilda was bequeathed into the care of the National Trust for Scotland. With ownership the Trust also inherited an existing agreement for the lease of three hectares of ground to the Royal Air Force for a radar base to track missiles from the recently developed rocket range on South Uist.

The base is still maintained on St Kilda and nothing can be done to camouflage its alien presence on Village Bay. An incongruous intrusion on the landscape to those approaching the island from the sea, it has nevertheless brought undeniable benefits – resident medical help, a helicopter pad and the generator which provides power for all on the island. Heat, light, and hot water are now available at the touch of a switch or the turn of a tap.

The National Trust for Scotland manages St Kilda in partnership with Scottish Natural Heritage, Historic Scotland, *Comhairle nan Eilean Siar* (the Western Isles Council), and the Ministry of Defence. The uniqueness of the jewel in their keeping was first acknowledged internationally in 1987 when the St Kilda archipelago was designated a World Heritage Site – one of only four in Scotland – for its spectacular natural features and the particular importance of its sea-bird colonies.

Further distinctions followed as St Kilda became a National Nature Reserve, a National Scenic Area, and a Site of Special Scientific Interest. In 2004 a successful application was made to have the World Heritage Site extended to include the surrounding marine environment. A year later Dual World Heritage Status was conferred by UNESCO in recognition of the island's unique cultural landscape, as outstanding as its natural attributes. St Kilda now ranks with such iconic places as Ayers Rock in Australia, Mount Athos in Greece, and the ancient Inca sanctuary of Machu Picchu in Peru.

As St Kilda's fame has spread it has become an increasingly popular destination for tourists and in 2008 it attracted 3,000 visitors, the highest number ever recorded. Fifteen cruise ships called and regular trips to the island from Lewis and Harris were often over-subscribed. A television documentary about the island resulted in a quarter of a million hits on the NTS St Kilda website.

The desire to visit St Kilda is nothing new, despite the physical difficulty of getting there. Archaeologists, peeling back the layers of the island's history, have found evidence of human occupation for at least the past 2,000 years and visitations to the island for the past 5,000 years. A wealth of evidence from the 15th century onwards reveals a rich island culture of literature, song, poetry, and folklore.

St Kilda may have been on the edge of the world but it was not beyond the pale of civilisation. Even Lady Grange in her time became aware of that. On her better days she would ask St Kildan girls to come and dance before her and, having learned some Gaelic, she is said to have listened with pleasure to the folk-tales and romances of the island. It would seem that even in her darkest moments, there were shafts of light for Rachel Chiesley too on the island of St Kilda.

The Grange Portrait Painters

SIR JOHN BAPTISTE DE MEDINA (1659–1710) was born in Brussels, the son of a Spanish sea captain. By 1686 he was established in London, where some of his Scottish patrons pointed out that a move to Edinburgh would provide him with as much work and less competition. Medina decided to take their advice, securing commissions in advance for 20 full-length and 40 half-length portraits. He took north with him a number of canvasses with the draperies already painted. All that was then required to individualise the portrait was the addition of the sitter's head and neck. Many of Medina's portraits still hang on the walls of Scotland's grand houses and historic institutions. He became a naturalised Scot and was knighted in 1707, the last man to be so honoured by the Scottish Parliament. The oil on canvas of Lady Grange attributed to him was painted c.1710.

WILLIAM AIKMAN (1682–1731), the son and heir of an Angus laird, enjoyed connections to the right people, in particular his uncle, Sir John Clerk of Penicuik. Aikman was already gainfully employed as a painter in Edinburgh in 1703, when he was only 21. He later left the city to spend time in London and Italy, returning in March 1711. The timing was fortuitous, or possibly deliberate, as Medina had died the previous October and Aikman slipped into the vacant position as visual recorder of the Scottish great and good. In 1722 he moved to London, two years after completing his portrait of Lord Grange. One of his last Scottish portraits must have been that of Allan Ramsay, which hangs today in the Scottish National Portrait Gallery. Ramsay was the best-known Scottish poet of the period and father to the even more famous painter of the same name. Aikman made only one brief visit back to Edinburgh – in 1730, the year before his death.

Lady Grange's Letters from St Kilda

FOLDED INTO VOLUME 10 of the *Proceedings of the Society of Antiquaries of Scotland* for 1872–73 is a facsimile of part of the original letter written by Lady Grange from St Kilda, dated 20 January 1738. The actual letter was then in the possession of the antiquarian David Laing who reported to a meeting of the Society in 1874 that it was one of several which had fallen into his hands 'unexpectedly, and not at one time.' This is the letter addressed to Charles Erskine, Solicitor General.

Where had it been since its arrival in Edinburgh in early December 1740? And who had carefully preserved it? How did it come to fall unexpectedly into the hands of David Laing? Unfortunately Laing does not answer these questions but we can still be grateful that we have the letter, which is held today in the Laing Collection in the University of Edinburgh Library. The complete text is printed in both Volume 10 and Volume 11 of the *Proceedings*. There had apparently been a problem with the printing in Volume 10 and Laing thought it advisable to reprint the letter, together with a revised commentary from himself, as an appendix to Volume 11. The facsimile, however, appears only in Volume 10.

The faintness of the ink and the folds of the paper made it impracticable to make a good facsimile of the whole letter. He reproduces only the well-spaced opening lines, full of flattery and religious references, and the final crushed lines as Lady Grange makes the most of the remaining space for a last desperate appeal to be rescued. However, the whole of the original letter is legible, despite Laing's reservations. It consists of two leaves of paper, slightly longer than an A4 sheet.

Also included in Laing's unexpected windfall was a copy of the second St Kilda letter of January 21, 1741, also held in the Laing Collection. The original does not seem to have survived. It would be distinguished by being in two distinct hands – the first and much greater part written by Roderick MacLennan, the second by Lady Grange. Fortunately a sufficient number of those who first received it responded to Lady Grange's request to 'write it over in a fair hand, and to shew it to all my friends' and at least two copies are still in existence. The copy in the Laing Collection is undated and not addressed to any specific person. A note, probably by Laing, suggests it could be the fair copy sent to the Reverend William Carlyle, minister of Prestonpans, the father of Dr Alexander Carlyle 'in whose repositories this imperfect Copy was found'.

The copy in the Laing Collection is indeed imperfect. Originally it had consisted of five leaves or ten pages, of the same size as the 1738 letter, but the third leaf (pages five and six) is missing. There is an undated scribble – '5th and 6th are wanting' – at the bottom of page four. The text of the missing section has been supplied from the first published copy, which appeared in the *Edinburgh Magazine and Literary Miscellany* for November 1817. This information is provided in a note dated 1850, doubtless also by Laing. Another copy, in the Scottish National Archives, runs to 18 pages, some of which are slightly damaged, but the letter is easily read as the writing is very clear.

An individual identified only as 'Gael' was responsible for the appearance in print in the *Edinburgh Magazine* of Lady Grange's second letter. Gael writes that the copy provided for the reproduction was found among the papers of someone who 'flourished at the time of the transaction to which it refers and who never would have put into his repository anything of that kind which was not authentic'. This sounds like a reference to Alexander Carlyle, and produces its own little puzzle. If Gael was using Carlyle's 'imperfect' copy in 1817, where did he get the text for the missing pages which would later, as the note in the Laing Collection claims, be used to complete the Carlyle copy? The most likely answer is that Gael had access to more than one copy of the letter. He himself claims that there were other copies in existence. He may have seen the original, for he refers to the point when the writing changes from MacLennan's to Lady Grange's. Gael adds the further intriguing information that some original letters of Lady Grange had recently been purchased from a respectable bookseller in Edinburgh 'for the purpose of destroying them'.

A reprint of the Gael article, with notes by James Maidment, appears in Richard Augustin Hay's *Genealogie of the Hayes of Tweeddale* (1835). Maidment identifies the 'respectable bookseller' as William Blackwood and the purchaser of the letters as John Francis, Earl of Mar, who had not destroyed them but presented them to the Marquess of Bute. The letters were then believed to be 'in the collection at Luton'.

Laing in his turn had no problem in identifying Gael. Unless he was mistaken (and Laing, with some justification, felt he rarely was) Gael was Sir George Stuart Mackenzie of Coull, who had visited St Kilda in 1800.

Thanks to the combined efforts of Gael, Maidment and Laing, we have the complete texts of both letters available in print plus the original 1738 letter and at least two contemporary fair copies of the second letter. Against all the odds Lady Grange did succeed in communicating back to the world, even if she never had the satisfaction of knowing this. By the survival of her letters she continues to do so.

Full Text of Lady Grange's Letter to Charles Erskine

LADY GRANGE'S LETTER from St Kilda to the Solicitor General shocks with its detailed account of her suffering and it is unambiguous in its demand for justice. Why the recipient – by then holding the powerful legal position of Lord Advocate – failed to react is one of the many enigmas in the Lady Grange story.

St Kilda, Jan. 1738

Sir – It is a great blessing and happiness to a nation when the King imployeth such a man as you are to Act and do for him who I'm perswadid his the aw and fear of God on him. Job was a just man and a perfect and the cause that he know not he searched out to deliver the poor and oppressed and him that had none to help him, a Patterne for on in your office. I have the Honour to be your Relation and I know you have much interest with Lord Greange if you can make Peace for me you know the promises that is to the peace maker; you know I'm not guilty of any crime except that of loveing my husband to much, he knows very well that he was my idol and now God his made him a rode to scourgeth me. Most just, you know he took a dislike and a hatred to poor unfortunat me can a woman get or ask better security of a Man then Vows and Oaths from a man of Conscience and Honour that tho he had swearen to his own hurt yet changeth not, he told me he loved me two years or he gott me and we lived 25 years together few or non I thought so happy there is no person but his a fault but ought he not to forgive me as he desires or expects to be forgiven of God, his heart I know is in God's hand and I know he can turne it as he Pleaseth. I know he will do much be the advices of friends. I pray God to incline your hearts to intercess'd for me, non on earth his so much power with Ld Grange as Lord Dun and you have if you both favour me I hope it will do. Make my compliments to Ld Dun I would have written to him but I want paper I'm sorrow for the great losses that his been in his family since I had the Honour to see him last you may remember you heard the Queen of Spain was put in prison and the Princess Sobeseke went to a Monastre you heard the reason of both no doubt and yet the Pope and other friends made Peace for them if friends take paines the same blessing may happen to me I'm sure you cannot but see how great a dishonour and blot it will leave on his memorie. But if friends can not prevaile with Ld Greange then let me have the Benefit of the law it is impossible for me to write or for you to imagine all the miserie and sorrow and hunger and cold and hardships of all kindes that I have suffer'd since I was stolen, if my paper allowed me I would give a particular account of the way, but I must be short and I have a bad pin, upon the 22^d of Jan 1732, I lodged in Margaret McLean house and a little before twelve at night Mrs McLean being on the plot opened the door and there rush'd in to my room some servants of Lovals and his Couson Roderick MacLeod he is a writter to the Signet they threw me down upon the floor in a Barbarous manner I cri'd murther murther then they stopp'd my mouth I puled out the cloth and told Rod:MacLeod I knew him their hard rude hands bleed and abased my face all below my eyes they dung out some of my teeth and toere the cloth of my head and toere out some of my hair I wrestled and defend'd my self with my hands then Rod: order'd to tye down my hands and cover my face most pitifully there was no skin left on my face with a cloath and stopp'd my mouth again they had wrestl'd so long with me that it was all that I could breath, then they carry'd me down stairs as a corps at the stair-foot they had a Chair and Alexander Foster of Carsbonny in the Chair who took me on his knee I made all the struggle I could but he held me fast in his arms my mouth being stopp'd I could not cry they carr'd me off very quickly without the Ports, when they open'd the Chair and took the cloath of my head I saw I was near to the Mutters of hill it being moonlight; I then show'd them that all the linnins about me were cover'd with blood. They had there about 6 or 7 horses they set me on a horses' behind Mr Foster and tyed me fast with a cloath to him that I might not leope of. if I remember right it was Peter Fraser Ld Lovaels page that set me on the horse, Rod:MacLeod and Ld Lovaets tenants rode along with me and Andrew Leishman come attending Mr Foster he is a servant in Wester Pomeis he knows the names of Lovaets Ser: we rode all night it being Saturday we mett no body or day breakes they took me into a house which belongs to John MacLeod advocate a little beyond Lithgow, I saw in that house a Gardener a Ser: of Johns and a Ser: of Alex: MacLeod advocate but I'm not sure if he was his first or his second man. They keep me there all day at night I was set on a horse behind Mr Foster they rode with me to Wester Pomeis it belongs to M Stewart and Mr Foster is his Factore he took me to the house of Pomeise thro a vault to a low room all the windows nailed up with thick board and no light in the room he was soo cruel as to

leave me all aloan and two doors lock'd on me, a Ser: of Ld Lov: kept
the keys of my prison James Fraser, And: Leishman mention'd before
is a tennant in Pomeise near thirtie years he brought what meat and
drink I got and his Wife mead my bed and wash'd my linens. I was
kept so close I grew sick then And: told Mr Foster he would not have
a hand in my death then I was allow'd to the court to get the Air I
then saw a son and three daughter which this Wife his born to And: I
told them I was Ld Grange Wife in hopes they would lett it be
knowen for Mr Fos:kept a gar'ner (George Rate) and his Wife in the
house that what provisions came might pass as to them he had a meal
yeard and house in Stirlin, they had two sons and a daughter come
often to see them I give them some thing to tell the ministers of Stirlin
Hamilton and Erskine that I was a prissonr in Pomeise but all in vain.
I was their near seven moneth Aug 15 Peter Fraser Ld Lov: page came
and three men with him. I had kept my bed all that day with grief and
sorrow Peter and James Fraser tho I was naked took me up by force
they set me on a horse behind Mr Foster I fainted dead with grief as
they set me on the horse, And: Leishman rode that nights journey with
me, whenever I cri'd they came to stope my mouth, they rode to the
highlands with me our guide a Servant of Sir Alexander Macdonald
Ronall Macdonald he since marr'd to Lady Macdonald own woman.
We rode all night or day breaks they took me in to a little house Mr
Foster never came near me after that night , but left the charge of me
to Lov:Servants I saw Rod:MacLeod at that house and a servant of his
Duncan Swine since that bond apprentice to a wright in or about
Edin' Mr Foster and Rod:MacLeod rode a parte of the way with us I
was set on a horse behind that vil'd paest fellow James Fraser, I can
not write the anguish and sorrow I was in I never read or hear'd of
any Wife whatever was her crime so cruely and barbarously treatt as I
have been. Peter and James Fraser left me with the three men that
came to Pomeise for me and two other came one of them belong'd to
Ld Lov. two days after we came to a Loch on Glangerry ground
Lochnern they had a sloop waiting there for me. The master of the
sloop told me he had been with Rod:MacLeod, he order'd him to take
me home to his own house and keeps me till farther orders they met in
Scotoss, he is uncle to this Glangerry his wife Rod: Aunt Scotass Sons
Ronald and John came to the sloop and saw me on Sep 30 we came to
the Isle Huskre it belongs to Sir Alexander Macdonald and this man is
the tannent, after I was some time there he thought it was a sin to
keep me he said he would let me go for tho Sir Alex: should take the
Isle from him he could not take his life. I sent a man for a boat and he

ran away with my money. In Jun: 1734 Rod: sent for the tanant of this Isle his name Alex.Macdonald to come to the Captain of Clan Ronalds house he told him I was to be taken from him. On the 14 of Jun: John MacLeod and his Brother Normand came with their Galley to the Huskre for me they were very rud and hurt me sore. Oh alas much have I suffer'd often my skin mead black and blew, they took me to St Kilda. John MacLeod is call'd Stewart of the Island he left me in a few days, no body lives in it but the poor natives it is a viled neasty stinking poor Isle I was in great miserie in the Husker but I am ten times worse and worse here, the Society sent a minister here I have given him a much fuller account then this and he wrat it down. You may be sure I have much more to tell then this. When this comes to you if you hear I'm alive do me justes and relieve me, I beg you make all hast but if you hear I'm dead do what you think right befor God.

> I am with great Respect
> your most humble servant
> but infortunat Cousen
> RACHELL ERSKINE

I pray you make my
Complements to all your
Young Family
  TO THE SOLICITOR

Select Bibliography

Printed Sources

Boswell, James *The Journal of a Tour to the Hebrides with Samuel Johnson*, London, 1785.

Buchan, Rev Alexander *A Description of St Kilda*, London, 1732.

Burnet, Bishop Gilbert *Bishop Gilbert Burnet's History of His Own Times*, London, posthumously published, 1734.

Campbell, JL *A Very Civil People: Hebridean Folk, History, and Tradition*, Edinburgh, 2000.

Carlyle, Rev Dr Alexander *Autobiography*, Edinburgh, 1860.

Clerk, Rev Archibald Clerk *New Statistical Account of Scotland*, vol. xiv, (Parish of Duirinish, Skye), Edinburgh and London, 1845.

Erskine, William *Epistle from Lady Grange to Edward D—, esq: written during her confinement in the Island of St. Kilda*, 1798.

Grant, Elizabeth *Memoirs of a Highland Lady*, Edinburgh, 1897.

Leneman, Leah *Alienated Affections: The Scottish Experience of Divorce and Separation 1684–1830*, Edinburgh, 1998.

Macaulay, Rev Kenneth *The History of St Kilda*, London, 1764.

MacCulloch, JA *The Misty Isle of Skye: Its Scenery, Its People, Its Story*, Edinburgh, 1905.

MacKinnon, Donald and Morrison, Alick *The MacLeods: The Genealogy of a Clan*, Edinburgh, 1968 (pp 32–34 for Roderick MacLeod).

Maclean, Charles *Island on the Edge of the World: Utopian St Kilda and its Passing*, London, 1972.

Maclean, Lachlan *Sketches of the Island of St Kilda*, Glasgow, 1838.

MacLeod, RC (ed.) *The Book of Dunvegan*, Spalding Club, Aberdeen, 1938 (for Charles MacSween's letter of 1763 and bills from Rory MacNeil to MacLeod for Lady Grange's board and lodgings, and funeral expenses).

Maidment, James (ed.) *Extracts from the Diary of a Senator of the College of Justice*, Edinburgh, 1843.

Martin, Martin *A Late Voyage to St Kilda*, London, 1698.

Nicolson, Alexander *History of Skye*, Glasgow, 1930.

Proceedings of the Society of Antiquaries of Scotland vols 10 and 11 for Laing's comments on documents now held in the Laing Collection, Edinburgh University Library. Volume 12 has the separation document, presented to the Society by Thomas Spowart.

Robson, Michael *St Kilda: Church, Visitors, and 'Natives'*, Port of Ness, 2005.

Scott, Sir Walter *The Bride of Lammermoor*, Edinburgh, 1819.

Sobieski Stuart, John and Charles Edward *Tales of the Century, or, Sketches of the Romance of History Between the Years 1746 and 1846*, Edinburgh, 1847.

Spalding Club Miscellany, vol. 3, 1846 for letters from Lord Grange to Thomas Erskine of Pittodry, 1731–33 and correspondence between Thomas Hope and Lord Grange, January and February 1741.

Steel, Tom *The Life and Death of St Kilda*, Glasgow, 1975.

Transactions of the Society of Antiquaries of Scotland, vol. 4, 1857, for Hay's Manuscript, with account of the murder of Sir George Lockhart.

Wodrow, Rev Robert *Analecta: or Materials for a History of Remarkable Providences; mostly relating to Scotch Ministers and Christians*, Maitland Club [Edinburgh], 1842.

Magazines and Journals

Edinburgh Journal, vol. 1, November, 1817, for the first printed copy of Lady Grange's second letter from St Kilda, provided by 'Gael'.

Chambers Edinburgh Journal, March 1846.

Chambers Magazine, July 1874.

Clan MacLeod Magazine, 1943 and 1957.

Manuscript Sources

Laing Collection, Special Collections Department, Edinburgh University Library (La.ll.201):

Lady Grange's two letters from St Kilda.

Separation agreement with signature of Lady Grange.

Lord Lovat's letters to Thomas Fraser, 7 June and 16 September 1732.

Original letter plus copy from Thomas Hope to Charles Erskine, 13 December 1740.

Memorial requesting a pension, from Thomas Hope to the King, 27 May 1761.

Mar and Kellie Papers, Scottish National Archives (GD124):

Erskine family correspondence.

Lord Grange's diary (used by Maidment).

Single-leaf copy of correspondence (1741) regarding the *Arabella* rescue attempt (copy by Lord Medwyn).

Unsigned letter, 20 April 1741, to John MacLeod from Lord Grange (copy by Lord Medwyn).

Lord Lovat's letter to Lord Grange, 12 October 1736.

Index

M

Macaulay, Rev Daniel, minister at
     Bracadale in Skye 103
Macdonald, Alexander, tacksman on
     Heskeir 81, 85, 86
MacDonald, Finlay, Lady Grange's
     guard on St Kilda 101, 109
Macdonell, Aeneas of Scothouse 89
Macdonell, John of Glengarry 89, 90
MacKenzie, Rev Neil, minister on St
     Kilda 110
MacLean, Lachlan, author of *Sketches
     of the Island of St Kilda* 109,
     110, 111
MacLennan, Mrs, wife of Roderick,
     minister on St Kilda 111, 117,
     125, 153
MacLennan, Rev Roderick 131, 178,
     179
  final years in the north 163, 164
  friendship with Lady Grange
     111-12
  minister on St Kilda 106, 113-18
  takes Lady Grange's letters to Edin-
     burgh 119, 121, 122
  transcription of one of Lady
     Grange's letters from St Kilda
     131
MacLeod, Donald, baron-bailie in
     Harris 106, 112, 127, 130
MacLeod, John of Muiravonside, ad-
     vocate 68, 89, 115, 116, 117,
     129, 131, 159
MacLeod, Norman, of Dunvegan,
     chief of the clan Macleod 62,
     85, 89, 141, 146, 147, 149
MacLeod, Roderick, advocate 65, 75,
     78, 89, 90, 159
Maidment, James 35, 88, 155, 156,
     169, 173, 180
Martin, Martin 91-98, 107, 108
Medina, John Baptiste de 16, 19, 177
Milltown 80, 81
Moidart, Loch 79

Monach Islands 84
Monro, Donald 84
Montagu, Lady Mary Wortley 58,
     62, 63

N

National Trust for Scotland 111, 175
Ness, Loch 80, 81, 90
Nevis, Loch 89

P

Pabbay, Island of 85, 86, 98, 100
Paterson, Lady Jean, sister of Lord
     Grange 54, 55, 153
Paterson, Sir Hugh of Bannockburn
     46, 53
Preston House 12, 34, 40, 41, 42,
     139, 142, 160

R

Royal Bounty Commission 163
Ruairidh Mhòr (Roderick the Imposter)
     95, 96-98

S

Scottish Society for the Propagation of
     Christian Knowledge (SSPCK)
     101, 103, 115, 116, 117, 118,
     163
Sheriffmuir, Battle of 20, 79, 136
Shiel, Loch 79
Sibbald, Sir Robert 93
Sir Walter Scott 29, 31
Skye, Isle of 11, 18, 69, 91, 92, 103,
     104, 115, 116, 159, 174
  Lady Grange on the island 141-47,
     149-151
Sobieski Stuart, John and Charles 51,
     54, 55, 57, 60, 64, 75, 79, 80,
     81, 85, 88, 90, 106, 107, 108,
     111, 113, 117, 131, 132, 145,
     161, 172
St Fillan's Pool 75, 78
St Giles 24, 25, 30, 101, 109

Riddoch on the Outer Hebrides
Lesley Riddoch
ISBN 1 906307 86 5 PBK £12.99

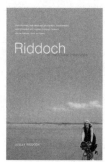

Riddoch on the Outer Hebrides is a thought-provoking commentary based on broadcaster Lesley Riddoch's cycle journey through a beautiful island chain facing seismic cultural and economic change. Her experience is described in a typically affectionate but hard-hitting style; with humour, anecdote and a growing sympathy for islanders tired of living at the margins but wary of closer contact with mainland Scotland.

Let's be proud of standing on the outer edge of a crazy mainstream world – when the centre collapses, the periphery becomes central. ALISTAIR MCINTOSH

She has a way of shining the magnifying glass on a well-documented place in a new and exciting way matching every beauty with a cultural wart that builds to create one of the most unfalteringly real images of the islands – all the more astounding for coming from an outsider. STORNOWAY GAZETTE

Lewis & Harris: History and Pre-History
Francis Thompson
ISBN 0 946487 77 4 PBK £5.99

The fierce Norsemen, intrepid missionaries and mighty Scottish clans – all have left a visible mark on the landscape of Lewis and Harris. This comprehensive guide explores sites of interest in the Western Isles, from prehistory through to the present day.

Harsh conditions failed to deter invaders from besieging these islands or intrepid travellers from settling, and their legacy has stood the test of time in an array of captivating archaeological remains from the stunningly preserved Carloway Broch, to a number of haunting standing stones, tombs and cairns. With captivating tales – including an intriguing murder mystery and a romantic encounter resulting in dramatic repercussions for warring clans – Francis Thompson introduces us to his homeland and gives us an insight into its forgotten ways of life.

Luath Press Limited

committed to publishing well written books worth reading

LUATH PRESS takes its name from Robert Burns, whose little collie
Luath (*Gael.*, swift or nimble) tripped up Jean Armour at a wedding
and gave him the chance to speak to the woman who was to be his wife
and the abiding love of his life. Burns called one of the 'Twa Dogs'
Luath after Cuchullin's hunting dog in Ossian's *Fingal*.
Luath Press was established in 1981 in the heart of
Burns country, and is now based a few steps up
the road from Burns' first lodgings on
Edinburgh's Royal Mile. Luath offers you
distinctive writing with a hint of
unexpected pleasures.
Most bookshops in the UK, the US, Canada,
Australia, New Zealand and parts of Europe,
either carry our books in stock or can order them
for you. To order direct from us, please send a £sterling
cheque, postal order, international money order or your
credit card details (number, address of cardholder and
expiry date) to us at the address below. Please add post
and packing as follows: UK – £1.00 per delivery address;
overseas surface mail – £2.50 per delivery address; overseas airmail
– £3.50 for the first book to each delivery address, plus £1.00 for each
additional book by airmail to the same address. If your order is a gift,
we will happily enclose your card or message at no extra charge.

Luath Press Limited

543/2 Castlehill
The Royal Mile
Edinburgh EH1 2ND
Scotland
Telephone: +44 (0)131 225 4326 (24 hours)
Fax: +44 (0)131 225 4324
email: sales@luath. co.uk
Website: www. luath.co.uk